D0478154

WRITERS
EXPRESS

A Handbook for
YOUNG WRITERS,
THINKERS, and LEARNERS

Teacher's Guide
to the handbook

. . . a teacher's guide to accompany

WRITERS
EXPRESS

WRITE SOURCE®

GREAT SOURCE EDUCATION GROUP
a Houghton Mifflin Company
Wilmington, Massachusetts
www.greatsource.com

About the
Teacher's Guide

The Teacher's Guide will help you use the *Writers Express* handbook effectively in your classroom, and it will also give you many tips and techniques for working with young writers and learners. We have tried to address the "big questions" teachers are asking today in a way that will help you integrate your professional experience with current research.

If you have any questions, please call. (Use our toll-free number—1-800-289-4490.) We are always ready to help or receive feedback.

The Write Source/Great Source Education Group

Written and compiled by
Patrick Sebranek, Dave Kemper, and Verne Meyer
Contributors and consultants: Laura Bachman, Carol Elsholz, Pat Kornelis, Lois Krenzke, Candyce Norvell, Kelly Brecher Saaf, Lester Smith, Vicki Spandel, Claire Ziffer

Printed in the United States of America

International Standard Book Number: 0-669-47166-6

1 2 3 4 5 6 7 8 9 10 -DBH- 04 03 02 01 00

Table of Contents

A Quick Tour of the Handbook

Writers Express serves as the perfect language handbook for grades 4 and 5, one that will help your students improve their ability **to write** (prewriting through publishing), **to think** (creatively, logically, clearly), and **to learn** (in the classroom, in small groups, independently). This quick tour highlights the five main sections of the handbook.

1 The Process of Writing

Students will use this part of the handbook to learn all about the writing process, from choosing a subject to learning about the traits of good writing, from writing with computers to developing persuasive essays.

Colorful illustrations and a personal tone make *Writers Express* very attractive to students.

24

Writing with Computers

Tools of the Trade

People can't work or play without the right tools. A family doctor couldn't examine a patient without a stethoscope or tongue depressor. (Say ahhh!) A mechanic without socket wrenches and screwdrivers might as well close up shop. And a spelunker, someone who explores caves, would be lost without a flashlight and hardhat.

All "Keyed Up"

One tool that many writers could not do without is the **personal computer.** Writers will tell you that a computer allows them to say a lot in a short amount of time. They will also tell you that revising and editing first drafts is easier on the computer.

> Remember the golden rule of the computer age: "Always save your work!"

Traits of Effective Writing **23**

Checklist for Good Writing

How can you tell if something you read or write has the traits of effective writing? You can use the following checklist.

✔ **Stimulating Ideas**
___ Did I present important, interesting information?
___ Did I hold the reader's attention all the way through?

✔ **Logical Organization**
___ Did I include a clear beginning, middle, and e
___ Did I use specific details to support the main i

✔ **Personal Voice**
___ Did I show my enthusiasm for the topic?
___ Is my writing easy to read aloud or listen to?

✔ **Original Word Choice**
___ Did I use strong verbs, specific nouns, and col
adjectives?
___ Did I help the reader picture what I am writin
about?

✔ **Smooth Sentences**
___ Did I mix short sentences with longer ones?
___ Did I show variety in my sentence beginnings?

✔ **Correct, Accurate Copy**
___ Did I follow the basic rules of spelling, capitali
grammar, and punctuation?

One Writer's Process **15**

Revising Improving the Writing

After reading over her first draft, Hillary tried to make her writing clearer and more complete. (The comments written in blue were made by a classmate.)

> A Great Teacher
>
> **Hillary rewords the first sentence.**
> Who is
> ~~Funny, helpful, and friendly,~~ what am I
> my my
> describing? Is it one of ~~your~~ classmates or ~~your~~
> my math
> best friend? Beleive it or not, I'm describing a
> teacher! His name is Mr. Vetter. We call him Mr. V.
>
> **She follows the advice of her writing partner (in blue).**
> One thing that I really like about him is the way
> he makes learning fun. Why is this
> sentence all alone?
> If math seams boring, he will make it fun by
> we
> **She rewrites a wordy sentence.**
> saying something ~~that is so funny so~~ you want to
> learn. Once I sneezed really loud in the middle
> of class. Right away, Mr. V. said "googolplex." It
> sounded just the same as gesundheit or bless you.
> Good example!
> Mr. V. is also . . .

Helpful checklists, guidelines, and student samples make information easy to use.

2 The Forms of Writing

In the "Forms of Writing" section, students will find guidelines and samples for personal narratives, book reviews, biographical stories, news stories, summaries, classroom reports, and much more.

158

The Parts of a Reporter

Eyes to see interesting details →

A curious mind to think of story ideas

A nose for news →

← Ears to listen for great quotations

A mouth to ask the right questions →

← A heart for understanding people

↖ Hands for writing down careful notes

Feet for following up on good stories ↘

220

Writing Realistic Stories

Amanda Comes to Life

Amanda Lowe is 10 years old. She has three big brothers who love to tease her. Her wildly curling red hair matches her fiery temper. Amanda sounds like a real person, but she isn't. She is a character in Cassie Johnson's realistic story.

What Are Realistic Stories?

Realistic stories are part real and part made-up. They usually have characters, like Amanda, who remind you of people you know. These characters have realistic problems to solve. For example, Amanda has a problem with her brothers, which is a believable problem for a 10-year-old girl. Made-up details and events add suspense or humor to the story.

Ideas for realistic stories often come from a writer's own experiences and interests. The finished products, though, are more fiction (made-up) than fact.

***Writers Express* addresses many forms of personal, subject, workplace, report, and creative writing.**

176

Business Writing

When You Mean Business

A very common form of writing used in the business world is the business letter. You will want to write business letters when

- **you need information (a letter of request),**
- **you have a problem with a service or a product (a letter of complaint), or**
- **you need to react to a situation in your city or school (a letter to an editor or official).**

Other common forms of business writing include memos and e-mail messages. You will learn about the special format for the business letter and the memo in this chapter. (**SEE** pages 146-147 for information about e-mail messages.)

3 The Tools of Learning

When students have a question about studying, reading, researching, or thinking, they should turn to this part of the handbook for help.

288

Building Vocabulary Skills

The Tools You Need

Think of your vocabulary as the tools you need for reading, writing, and talking. The more tools you have, the more you can do with language.

Suppose your friend Sean says to you, "Jim *donated* $10 for our clubhouse, but now he says he only *lent* us the money!" If you don't know what *donated* and *lent* mean, you won't know why your friend is upset. But if *donated* and *lent* are in your "word toolbox," you'll understand: Sean thought the money was a *gift*, but Jim is telling Sean he has to *pay it back*.

> Wonderful, wild, and whimsical words wander in and out of the world of writers.

***Writers Express* makes all aspects of language and learning active, enjoyable, and meaningful.**

334

Kinds of Graphics

Graphic organizers come in many different shapes and sizes. On these two pages you'll find some common graphic organizers and tips on when to use them.

Web Organizer •
Use a web whenever you gather facts or respond to reports, personal narratives, stories, and poems.

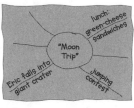

"Moon Trip"
lunch: green-cheese sandwiches
jumping contest
Eric falls into giant crater

5 W's Organizer •
Use the 5 W's whenever you gather details for newspaper stories, personal narratives, and fictional stories.

who? — Lakewood High School girls' soccer team
what? — won the state soccer championship
when? — yesterday
where? — Florida state soccer tournament
why? — team played excellent defense
(News Story)

Helpful Hint: (**SEE** page 161 for a sample news story.)

5 Senses Organizer • Use it whenever you gather details for observation reports and descriptive paragraphs.

Sight	Sound	Smell	Taste	Touch
bright Ferris wheel	people laughing	popcorn	nachos with warm cheese	Carmen spilled wet, sticky cold on me

358

Managing Your Time

If you're like most students, you have a limited amount of time, and lots of things to do. The best way to make sure you get everything done is to use a planner.

Daily Planner • In a daily planner you can list assignments you have for each day. Your planner may be a simple list.

■ MONDAY, _____ (date)

English
Read page 102. Write a topic sentence.

Math
Do workbook page 16. (Test tomorrow)

Social Studies
Answer question sheet by Wednesday.

■ TUESDAY, _____ (date)

English
Write a paragraph using my topic sentence.

Social Studies
Finish question sheet for tomorrow.

Science
Collect five different leaves; take to class.

Weekly Planner • A weekly planner is a schedule of all the important things you have to do during a week.

Day	Before School	School	After School	Evening
Mon.	Make lunch for field trip	Field trip	Open gym	Study math
Tues.	Take garbage out	Math test	Do homework	Choir practice

4 Proofreader's Guide

Whenever students have a question about punctuation, capitalization, usage, and the parts of speech, send them to this color-coded (yellow) section of the handbook.

390

Capitalization (continued)

Geographic Names	Capitalize geographic names that are either proper nouns or proper adjectives.
	Planets and heavenly bodies . . . . **Earth, Jupiter, Milky Way**
	Continents . . . . **Europe, Asia, South America, Australia, Africa**
	Countries . . . . **Chad, Haiti, Greece, Chile, Jordan**
	States . . . . **New Mexico, Alabama, West Virginia, Delaware, Iowa**
	Provinces . . . . **Alberta, British Columbia, Québec, Ontario**
	Cities . . . . **Montreal, Portland**
	Counties . . . . **Wayne County, Dade County**
	Bodies of water . . . . **Hudson Bay, North Sea, Lake Geneva, Saskatchewan River, Indian Ocean, Gulf of Mexico**
	Landforms . . . . **Appalachian Mountains, Bitterroot Range, Capitol Reef**
	Public areas . . . . **Vietnam Memorial, Sequoia National Forest**
	Roads and highways . . . . **New Jersey Turnpike, Interstate 80, Central Avenue, Adam's Apple Road**
	Buildings . . . . **Pentagon, Oriental Theater, Empire State Building**

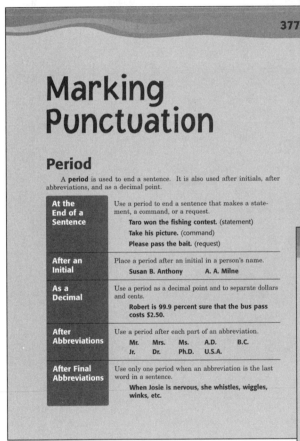

377

Marking Punctuation

Period

A **period** is used to end a sentence. It is also used after initials, after abbreviations, and as a decimal point.

At the End of a Sentence	Use a period to end a sentence that makes a statement, a command, or a request.
	Taro won the fishing contest. (statement)
	Take his picture. (command)
	Please pass the bait. (request)
After an Initial	Place a period after an initial in a person's name.
	Susan B. Anthony **A. A. Milne**
As a Decimal	Use a period as a decimal point and to separate dollars and cents.
	Robert is 99.9 percent sure that the bus pass costs $2.50.
After Abbreviations	Use a period after each part of an abbreviation.
	Mr. **Mrs.** **Ms.** **A.D.** **B.C.**
	Jr. **Dr.** **Ph.D.** **U.S.A.**
After Final Abbreviations	Use only one period when an abbreviation is the last word in a sentence.
	When Josie is nervous, she whistles, wiggles, winks, etc.

This easy-to-use guide answers all your students' editing and proofreading questions.

402

Using the Right Word

You need to use "the right words" in your writing and speaking, and this section will help you do that. First, look over the commonly misused words on the next 10 pages. Then, whenever you have a question about which word is the *right* word, come back to this section for help. (Remember to look for your word in a dictionary if you don't find it here.)

a, an	**I played a joke on my dad.** (Use *a* before words beginning with a consonant sound.)
	I placed an ugly rubber chicken under his pillow. (Use *an* before words beginning with a vowel sound.)
accept, except	**Please accept my apology.** (*Accept* means "to receive.")
	Everyone except me finished the race. (*Except* means "other than.")
allowed, aloud	**We are allowed to read to partners in class.** (*Allowed* means "permitted.")
	We may not read aloud in the library, however. (*Aloud* is an adverb meaning "clearly heard.")
a lot	**A lot of my friends like jeans with holes in them.** (*A lot* is always two words.)

5 Student Almanac

The last section contains a great deal of helpful information for students to use in all of their classes.

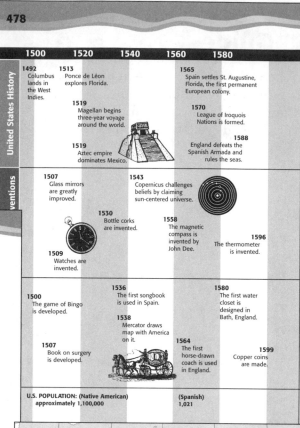

Making History

This section of your handbook includes a close look at the United States Constitution, a chart of presidents and vice presidents, and a historical time line.

The U.S. Constitution

Of the many history-making events in United States history, none is more important than the convention held in Philadelphia in 1787. It was held to revise the Articles of Confederation. Instead, the delegates decided to write a new plan for the government.

By the time the convention ended, George Washington and the other delegates had passed the United States Constitution. Through the years, this Constitution has been changed (amended) several times, but it is still the "law of the land," just as it was 200 years ago.

Full-color maps, a historical time line, the metric system— *Writers Express* **is truly an all-school handbook.**

Introducing the Handbook

The pages in this section can be used to introduce *Writers Express* to your students and get them started on the road to becoming active, independent learners.

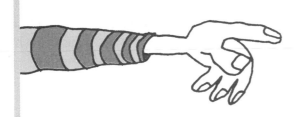

Getting-Started Activities

We created the *Writers Express* handbook with the goal of making it a handbook students would like and use every day. To make this a reality, students must first understand what's in the handbook and how they can use it. The activities that follow will introduce the handbook to your students and help them become proficient handbook users. (You will find the answer key for the getting-started activities on pages 16-17.)

Scavenger Hunts

One popular way to help students get to know the handbook is to create scavenger hunts, which basically ask students to find a random list of items in *Writers Express*. The scavenger hunts we have provided can be done in small groups or as a class. They are designed for oral answers, but you may want to have your students write answers. Also, you may want to have students take turns finding the items and then, on the next scavenger hunt, challenge students to "race" for the answers.

After your students have done a scavenger hunt, you can challenge them to create their own versions. For example, small groups can work together to create scavenger hunts and then exchange their "hunts" with other groups. Or, you may develop additional questions for students to answer using the handbook, and pattern this activity after a popular game show.

Other Activities

■ Design a Handbook

Before you even hand out *Writers Express,* ask students what they would put into an all-purpose student handbook if they were in charge of designing one. (Explain that a handbook is a book that can easily be carried as a ready reference. It generally covers one special subject—in this case language arts and writing.) They may come up with ideas like topics for writing, tips for taking a test, and so on. List their suggestions on the board or on an overhead. Then hand out *Writers Express* and ask students to review the handbook, noting how it matches up to the list on the board.

■ Favorite Feature

Give your students the following assignment: Find one page, one short section, one set of guidelines, one illustration, one writing sample, or one chart you think is interesting, entertaining, stimulating, valuable, etc. Students should prepare to share their discoveries with members of their discussion group or with the entire class.

■ The 5 W's and H

Have students develop *Who? What? When? Where? Why?* and *How?* questions from *Writers Express*. Students should then exchange questions with a partner and search for answers in the handbook. Upon completion, partners should read and react to each other's answers. This could also be used as a handbook search contest. For example: **What** is step one in the writing process?

■ All Classes

Have students list all their subjects (math, science, etc.) along the left-hand margin of a piece of paper. Then ask students to find information—chapters, checklists, pages, and so on—in *Writers Express* that would help them in each subject. Have students share their results with the class.

Your First Week with the Handbook

Resources: *Writers Express Handbook* (HB), iii
Writers Express Teacher's Guide (TG), 8-18

Day 1

1. Pass out individual copies of *Writers Express*. Give students, in pairs, a few minutes to explore the handbook and talk about it.
2. Duplicate and distribute "Getting to Know My Handbook" (TG 10) or "*Writers Express* Letter Puzzle" (TG 11). Have students work with partners to complete the activity.

Day 2

1. Preview "Express Yourself!" (HB iii). Have students turn to the parts of the handbook that are mentioned on this page.
2. Continue with "Get Ready, Get Set, Go!" (TG 12) and "A Quick Tour" (TG 13).

Day 3

1. Continue with more getting-started activities (TG 8).
2. Then have students do "Scavenger Hunt A" (TG 14).

Day 4

1. Have students work on "Scavenger Hunt B" (TG 15).
2. Give students a few minutes to prepare for a class discussion the next day. Have them take notes and be prepared to share what they like about the handbook, how they plan to use it, and questions they have about it.

Day 5

1. Have a class discussion in which students share what they like about the handbook, how they plan to use it, and questions they have.
2. Try a couple of the minilessons (TG 18).

Note: Fill in, whenever you need to, with the "Other Activities" (TG 8) and the minilessons (TG 18).

Getting to Know My Handbook

Directions To complete this chart, you will have to find words from six different lists in *Writers Express*. (Use the index to find each list.) Make sure that the words you select begin with the letters in the left-hand column, and make sure that you spell these words correctly. (Two words have been filled in for you.)

	Commonly Misspelled Words (See "Spelling")	Writing Terms	Guidelines for Thinking and Writing	Usage and Commonly Misused Words	Countries I Have Never Seen (See "Maps")	Forms of Writing
E	electricity	editing				

EXPRESS Yourself!

P						
R						
E						
S						
S						

Writers Express **Letter Puzzle**

Directions Fill in the spaces with the letters described in the clues below to make a sentence.

___ ___ ___ ___ ___ ___ ___   ___ ___ ___ ___   ___ ___
1   2   3   4   3   5   6   7   8   4   9   10 8

___ ___ ___ ___ ___ ___ ___   ___ ___ ___ ___ ___ ___ ___!
8   11 12 2   8   9   9   10 13 9   8   7   14

1. First letter of the title of your handbook

2. First letter of a word that describes a special type of story (See page 220.)

3. The only one-letter personal pronoun (See page 422.)

4. The last letter of the last word on page 227

5. The letter at the top of a *compass rose* (See page 457.)

6. The first letter of a root word that means "write" (See page 300.)

7. The first letter in the name of a type of diagram that shows how things are organized into groups, like a family tree (See page 282.)

8. First letter of the second and third words in the title of the chapter that starts on page 88

9. The first letter of each word that names the fifth trait of good writing (See page 19.)

10. The first letter of a prefix that means "large" (See page 295.)

11. In the index to world maps (pages 469-471), this is the only letter with no country.

12. First letter of both words in the title of the chapter that starts on page 318

13. In a spelling rule, you change this letter to "i" and add *es* when you form a plural. (See page 309.)

14. The first letter of a four-letter word that describes something that is true (See page 347.)

Get Ready, Get Set, Go!

As you follow the directions below, you will learn about the first two sections in your handbook: "The Process of Writing" and "The Forms of Writing."

1. Turn to page 9 in your handbook and read about the five steps in the writing process. What are the first and last steps?

   _____

2. Look at page 30. What does a writer collect in a personal portfolio?

   _____

3. Read the descriptive paragraph on page 78. What title would you give it?

   _____

4. Review page 109. What are two kinds of narrative writing about a person?

   _____

5. Study page 114. What are the two basic parts of a sentence?

   _____

6. Look at the parts of a newspaper story on page 160. What is a *byline?*

   _____

7. Read Emery Sanford's science report on page 191. What is the most surprising fact you learned about the subject?

   _____

8. Make friends with the poem "Words" by following the steps on page 239.

A Quick Tour

Directions As you follow the directions below, you will learn about the last three sections in the handbook: "The Tools of Learning," "Proofreader's Guide," and "Student Almanac."

1. Identify two strategies for building your vocabulary (pages 289-294).

_____

2. Name three things to "watch for" when viewing the news (page 325).

_____

3. Study page 347. Find out the difference between a fact and an opinion. Then write one fact about *Writers Express*.

_____

4. Write your address in a sentence. Use commas correctly (page 379).

My address is _____

_____

5. Pretend you work at a Mexican restaurant and have an order for more than one burrito. How would you write the plural of *burrito* (page 394)?

_____

6. Decide if you write on *stationary* or *stationery* (page 410).

_____

7. During the 1960s, what year did men first walk on the moon (page 486)?

_____

Scavenger Hunt A

Using the table of contents in your handbook (pages iv-viii), write down the page number you would turn to if you were looking for the following types of information.

1. You want to know how to publish a piece of writing. _____

2. You are going to write a news story for your class newspaper. _____

3. You could use help studying for an important test. _____

4. You wonder where to put the commas when writing a date. _____

5. You want to know which U.S. president served the longest time. _____

Now, using the handbook index (pages 489-504), write down the page numbers and then answer the questions that follow.

1. Find a checklist for essays. page number: _____

   What is one thing you should check for? _____

2. Find information about alliteration. page number: _____

   What example is given? _____

3. Find information about graphs. page numbers: _____

   What is one type of graph? _____

4. Find a list of greetings in foreign languages. page number: _____

   How would you say "good-bye" in Thai? _____

5. Find a map of Asia. page number: _____

   What is one country that borders India? _____

Scavenger Hunt B

Using the table of contents in your handbook, write down the page number you would turn to if you were looking for the following types of information.

1. You want to combine some shorter sentences in a story. _____

2. You need to know how to summarize a magazine article you are reading

   for science class. _____

3. You want to become a better reader. _____

4. You want to use the right word—*to, too,* or *two.* _____

5. You're considering a new pet and wonder how long rabbits live. _____

Now, using the handbook index, write down the page numbers and answer the questions that follow.

1. Find the parts of a business letter. page numbers: _____

   What part includes the sender's address? _____

2. Find a checklist of the basics of life. page number: _____

   What is the first step in using the checklist?

   _____

3. Find information about television viewing. page numbers: _____

   On average, how many hours of TV do we watch each week? _____

4. Find information about punctuating titles. page numbers: _____

   What punctuation is used for the title of a song? _____

Answer Key

Getting to Know My Handbook

(Answers will vary.)

	Commonly Misspelled Words (See "Spelling")	Writing Terms	Guidelines for Thinking and Writing	Usage and Commonly Misused Words	Countries I Have Never Seen (See "Maps")	Forms of Writing
E	electricity	editing	explain	eight	Ecuador	e-mail

EXPRESS Yourself!

P	package	pun	predict	pore	Portugal	poems
R	receive	revising	rate	raise	Rwanda	reports
E	Easter	expository writing	evaluating	except	Ethiopia	editorials
S	shoes	slang	summarize	steal	Serbia	slogans
S	Sunday	style	solve	sew	Syria	songs

Writers Express Letter Puzzle

W	R	I	T	I	N	G		L	E	T	S		M	E
1	2	3	4	3	5	6		7	8	4	9		10	8

E	X	P	R	E	S	S		M	Y	S	E	L	F	!
8	11	12	2	8	9	9		10	13	9	8	7	14	

1. First letter of the title of your handbook
2. First letter of a word that describes a special type of story (See page 220.)
3. The only one-letter personal pronoun (See page 422.)
4. The last letter of the last word on page 227
5. The letter at the top of a *compass rose* (See page 457.)
6. The first letter of a root word that means "write" (See page 300.)
7. The first letter in the name of a type of diagram that shows how things are organized into groups, like a family tree (See page 282.)
8. First letter of the second and third words in the title of the chapter that starts on page 88
9. The first letter of each word that names the fifth trait of good writing (See page 19.)
10. The first letter of a prefix that means "large" (See page 295.)
11. In the index to world maps (pages 469-471), this is the only letter with no country
12. First letter of both words in the title of the chapter that starts on page 318
13. In a spelling rule, you change this letter to "i" and add *es* when you form a plural (See page 309.)
14. The first letter of a four-letter word that describes something that is true (See page 347.)

Get Ready, Get Set, Go!

1. Turn to page 9 in your handbook and read about the five steps in the writing process. What are the first and last steps?

   prewriting and publishing

2. Look at page 30. What does a writer collect in a personal portfolio?

   lists of new ideas, quotations, early drafts, and final copies

3. Read the descriptive paragraph on page 78. What title would you give it?

   (Answers will vary.)

4. Review page 109. What are two kinds of narrative writing about a person?

   autobiographical and biographical

5. Study page 114. What are the two basic parts of a sentence?

   the subject and the verb

6. Look at the parts of a newspaper story on page 160. What is a *byline?*

   the name of the writer of a story

7. Read Emery Sanford's science report on page 191. What is the most surprising fact you learned about the subject?

   (Answers will vary.)

8. Make friends with the poem "Words" by following the steps on page 239.

A Quick Tour

1. Identify two strategies for building your vocabulary (pages 289-294).

   read and check, use a dictionary, use a thesaurus, keep a personal dictionary, learn about word parts, watch for word families

2. Name three things to "watch for" when viewing the news (page 325).

   completeness, correctness, and balance

3. Study page 347. Find out the difference between a fact and an opinion. Then write one fact about *Writers Express.*

   (Answers will vary.)

4. Write your address in a sentence. Use commas correctly (page 379).

   My address is (Answers will vary.)

5. Pretend you work at a Mexican restaurant and have an order for more than one burrito. How would you write the plural of *burrito* (page 394)?

   burritos

6. Decide if you write on *stationary* or *stationery* (page 410).

   stationery

7. During the 1960s, what year did men first walk on the moon (page 486)?

   1969

Scavenger Hunt A

Directions Using the table of contents in your handbook (pages iv-viii), write down the page number you would turn to if you were looking for the following types of information.

1. You want to know how to publish a piece of writing. _68_

2. You are going to write a news story for your class newspaper. _156_

3. You could use help studying for an important test. _366_

4. You wonder where to put the commas when writing a date. _379_

5. You want to know which U.S. president served the longest time. _476_

Directions Now, using the handbook index (pages 489-504), write down the page numbers and then answer the questions that follow.

1. Find a checklist for essays. page number: _111_
What is one thing you should check for? _purpose, audience, voice, beginning, middle, ending_

2. Find information about alliteration. page number: _245_
What example is given? _dance, dare, and drop_

3. Find information about graphs. page numbers: _283-285_
What is one type of graph? _bar graph, line graph, or pie graph_

4. Find a list of greetings in foreign languages. page number: _439_
How would you say "good-bye" in Thai? _la kone na ka_

5. Find a map of Asia. page number: _467_
What is one country that borders India? _Pakistan, China, Nepal, Bhutan, Bangladesh, or Myanmar_

14

Scavenger Hunt B

Directions Using the table of contents in your handbook, write down the page number you would turn to if you were looking for the following types of information.

1. You want to combine some shorter sentences in a story. _118_

2. You need to know how to summarize a magazine article you are reading for science class. _185_

3. You want to become a better reader. _271_

4. You want to use the right word—*to, too,* or *two.* _402_

5. You're considering a new pet and wonder how long rabbits live. _442_

Directions Now, using the handbook index, write down the page numbers and answer the questions that follow.

1. Find the parts of a business letter. page numbers: _178-179_
What part includes the sender's address? _heading_

2. Find a checklist of the basics of life. page number: _37_
What is the first step in using the checklist?
Choose one of the categories or groups.

3. Find information about television viewing. page numbers: _324-328_
On average, how many hours of TV do we watch each week? _19 or 20_

4. Find information about punctuating titles. page numbers: _386, 388_
What punctuation is used for the title of a song? _quotation marks_

15

Minilessons for Using *Writers Express*

Directions Conduct minilessons on a regular basis to give your students practice using *Writers Express*. Use the samples below as a guide when you design your own minilessons. See pages 225-264 in this guide for additional minilessons.

That's so basic! .... Choosing a Subject

■ As a writing assignment, you've been asked to explain how to do or make something. **TURN** to "Using a Checklist" on handbook page 37 and **LIST** at least three subjects you could write about. (**SHARE** the results of your work.)

Follow a leader. .... Writing with Style

■ **PRACTICE** writing sentences modeled after two sentences (or short passages) in one of your favorite books. **USE** the guidelines and examples on handbook page 128 to help you complete your work. (**SHARE** your results.)

First Feelings .... Writing Book Reviews

■ **LEARN** about reader response journals on handbook page 171. Then **WRITE** four or five journal entries for the next book you read, using the "How to Respond" section as your guide. Try to write at least eight or nine lines each time you write.

Did you say "Quill"? .... Using Reading Strategies

■ **LEARN** about the KWL reading strategy on handbook page 273. Then **USE** the strategy as you read any chapter in *Writers Express*.

Study Time and Fun Time ..... Completing Assignments

■ **PLAN** your study time and fun time for the next week using the "Weekly Planner" chart on handbook page 358 as your guide. After the week is over, **WRITE** a journal entry exploring how the planner worked for you. (**SHARE** the results of your work.)

Using the Handbook in the Classroom

Where does *Writers Express* fit in?

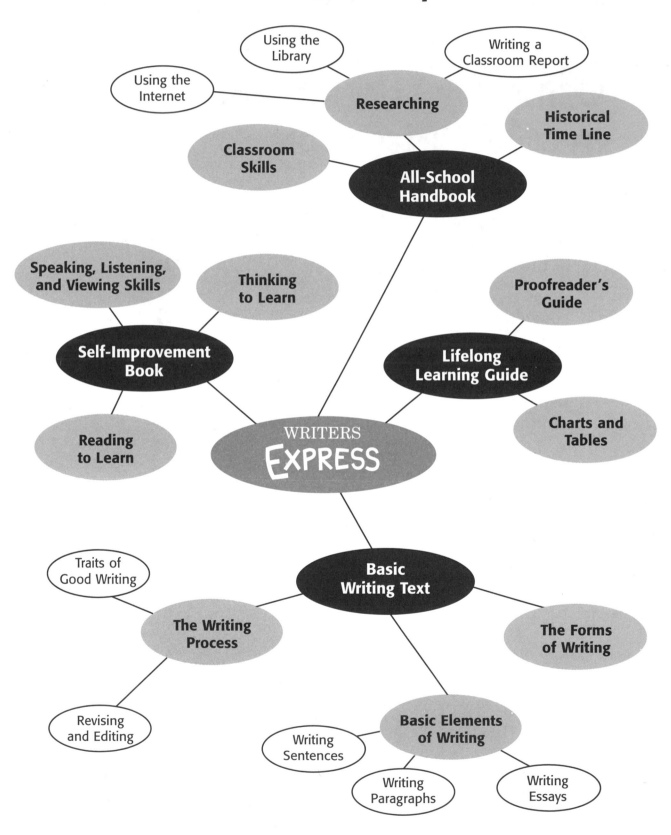

- Using the Library
- Writing a Classroom Report
- Using the Internet
- **Researching**
- **Historical Time Line**
- **Classroom Skills**
- **All-School Handbook**
- **Speaking, Listening, and Viewing Skills**
- **Thinking to Learn**
- **Proofreader's Guide**
- **Self-Improvement Book**
- **Lifelong Learning Guide**
- **Reading to Learn**
- WRITERS **EXPRESS**
- **Charts and Tables**
- Traits of Good Writing
- **Basic Writing Text**
- **The Writing Process**
- **The Forms of Writing**
- Revising and Editing
- **Basic Elements of Writing**
- Writing Sentences
- Writing Paragraphs
- Writing Essays

Using the *Writers Express* Handbook in the Language Arts Classroom

Q. Can teachers develop a language program with *Writers Express* and the *Teacher's Guide*?

A. Yes. These two resources can serve as the foundation for a language arts program promoting, among other things, student-centered language learning, writing as a process of discovery, and the reading-writing connection. These products can also serve as the foundation for a schoolwide writing and learning program.

Since *Writers Express* functions mainly as a writing handbook, that is where teachers should first focus their attention. These are two basic questions that should be answered during initial planning: **How will writing instruction be approached?** Will students engage in writing workshops? Will writing be integrated into thematic units? **What types of writing will be covered?** Will personal forms of writing be emphasized in grade 4? Will paragraphs be of primary importance in grade 5?

"Effective Writing Instruction," page 160 in this guide, will help teachers answer the first question. Teachers can answer the second question by reviewing the forms of writing covered in the handbook. (Refer to the framework of writing activities for grades 4 and 5 listed on page 22 in this guide.)

Q. What about learning and study skills?

A. In the "Learning Skills" section (handbook pages 353-375), teachers will find guidelines related to studying and learning. Perhaps writing to learn and note taking could be emphasized in one grade and test taking in the other.

Q. What about the other language arts?

A. Teachers will find major sections in the handbook related to searching, thinking, and reading skills.

Finding Information (pages 255-269)
Various primary and secondary sources can be emphasized at different grade levels. In addition, students can explore the Internet and the library in more depth from year to year.

Thinking Skills (pages 333-351)
This section addresses thinking from a number of different perspectives. The primary focus of attention in one grade might be recalling and understanding information; in another grade, applying and analyzing information; and so on.

Reading and Spelling Skills (pages 271-309)
A number of different patterns of nonfiction should be practiced at each grade level. We also suggest that the glossary of prefixes, suffixes, and roots should be the focus of vocabulary study. (See 295-304 in the handbook.)

Q. What else should teachers remember when planning with *Writers Express*?

A. Teachers should always remember to turn to the "Introductory Notes" in this teacher's guide (pages 31-158) whenever they are planning a unit around a particular chapter in the handbook.

What specific types of writing are covered in *Writers Express*?

The chart below lists the types of writing discussed in the *Writers Express* handbook. The types of writing are listed in this manner to indicate a possible framework or sequence of activities, moving from personal writing to writing that becomes more creative and reflective. Teachers can use this framework as a starting point when planning a writing program (or individual writing activities) with the handbook.

	Level 4	Level 5
PERSONAL WRITING		
Recording	Writing in Journals (133) Writing to Learn (42, 353)	Writing in Journals (133) Writing to Learn (42, 353)
Recalling and Remembering	Narrative Paragraph (79) Writing Personal Narratives (138)	Narrative Paragraph (79) Writing About an Event (110)
SUBJECT WRITING		
Introducing	Writing Family Stories (143)	Describing a Person (103)
Describing	Descriptive Paragraph (78) Writing Observation Reports (188)	Descriptive Paragraph (78) Writing About a Special Object (105)
Reporting	Writing Newspaper Stories (156)	Writing Newspaper Stories (156)
Corresponding	Writing Friendly Letters (144) Writing a Letter of Request (179)	Writing Friendly Letters (144) Writing a Letter of Complaint (180)
Informing	Expository Paragraph (80) Writing Explanations (172)	Expository Paragraph (80) Writing Informational Essays (88)
Searching and Researching	Writing a Summary (185)	Writing a Summary (185) Writing a Classroom Report (192)
CREATIVE WRITING		
Imagining	Writing Tall Tales (216) Writing Realistic Stories (220)	Writing Fantasies (209) Writing Stories from History (226)
Inventing	Writing a Free-Verse Poem (242) Playful Poetry (248) Writing Plays (232)	Writing a Free-Verse Poem (242) Traditional Poetry (246) Writing Riddles (250)
REFLECTIVE WRITING		
Applying and Analyzing	Applying Information (341) Comparing and Contrasting (335)	Cause and Effect Writing (335, 342) Problems and Solutions (351)
Persuading	Persuasive Paragraph (81)	Writing a Letter to the Editor (164, 176)
Reviewing	Writing a Brochure Book Review (170)	Writing Book Reviews (166)

How are the modes of writing covered in the handbook?

Many language arts curriculums approach writing according to the different modes of writing: *narrative, descriptive, expository,* and *persuasive.* The chart below shows how the modes of writing are covered in the *Writers Express* handbook. Teachers may find this chart helpful when planning writing assignments. Also see pages 41-42 in *Writers Express.*

Narrative

Biographical Writing **151-155**

Narrative Essay **106-111**

Narrative Paragraph **79**

Writing About an Event (Guidelines) **110**

Writing Fantasies **209-215**

Writing Friendly Notes and
    Letters **144-147**

Writing Personal Narratives **138-143**

Writing Plays **232-237**

Writing Realistic Stories **220-225**

Writing Stories from History **226-231**

Writing Tall Tales **216-219**

Descriptive

Biographical Writing **151-155**

Book Reviews **137, 166-171**

Character Sketch **152-155**

Describing a Person (Guidelines) **103**

Describing a Place (Guidelines) **104**

Describing an Object (Guidelines) **105**

Descriptive Paragraph **78**

Writing a Descriptive Essay **100-102**

Expository

Expository Paragraph **80**

How-To Writing **172-175**

Writing a Classroom Report **192-203**

Writing Expository Essays **88-93**

Multimedia Computer Reports **204-207**

Writing Newspaper Stories **156-165**

Writing Social Notes **148-149**

Writing Speeches **205-207, 311-317**

Writing Summaries **185-187**

Writing Business Letters **176-181**

Persuasive

Persuasive Paragraph **81, 344**

Writing Persuasive Essays **94-99**

Writing Letters to the Editor **164-165**

Writing Book Review Brochures **170**

Using the Handbook as an All-School Writing and Learning Guide

Because there is such a wide range of information covered in *Writers Express*, it can be used in many different ways. For example, in many schools the handbook serves as an **all-school resource**—one that students refer to in every class for help with their writing, study-reading, note taking, test taking, and so on. Once teachers in all subject areas become familiar with the contents of the handbook, they will understand its potential as a writing and learning tool. The following list demonstrates the handbook's cross-curricular value.

Special Note: See "Writing Throughout the Day" on pages 169-178 in this guide for more information about writing across the curriculum.

Writing Skills

- Why Write? (1)
- A Basic Writing Guide (3-7)
- Steps in the Writing Process (8-11)
- Writing with Computers (24-29)
- Organize Your Details (48)
- Writing Paragraphs (75-84)
- Transition Words (85)
- Writing Expository Essays (88-93)
- Writing Persuasive Essays (94-99)
- Business Writing (176-183)
- Thinking and Writing (338-345)
- Thinking Clearly (346-351)
- Writing as a Learning Tool (353-355)

Researching Skills

- Research Your Subject (46)
- Writing Observation Reports (188-191)
- Writing a Summary (185-187)
- Writing a Classroom Report (192-203)
- Multimedia Computer Reports (204-207)
- Using the Internet (264-269)
- Using the Library (255-263)

Reading and Speaking Skills

- Using Reading Strategies (271-279)
- Reading Graphics (280-287)
- Building Vocabulary Skills (288-305)
- Giving Speeches (311-317)
- Performing Poems (318-323)

Study Skills

- Improving Viewing Skills (324-329)
- Improving Listening Skills (330-331)
- Completing Assignments (356-359)
- Working in Groups (360-365)
- Taking Tests (366-373)
- Taking Good Notes (374-375)

Helpful Charts and Lists

- Periodic Table of the Elements (443)
- The Metric System (446-448)
- Math Symbols, Numbers, and Tables (454-455)
- Maps (459-468)
- Government (472-477)
- Historical Time Line (478-487)

Using the Handbook for Standards-Based Instruction

Today, teachers are expected to use standards to inform instruction. Standards are the tools used to justify and document what is being taught and what students are achieving. As you will see on the next four pages, *Writers Express* can serve as an important resource for planning instruction that meets the essential *writing standards* as developed at the national, state, and/or local level. (The performance standards that follow reflect the writing skills and forms that students should understand and employ by grade 5.)

The Process of Writing

Understanding How Writing Works

The student is expected to . . .   Handbook Pages

• **use** prewriting strategies such as brainstorming, freewriting, graphic organizers (clusters and webs), lists, notes, and logs to collect, generate, and organize ideas.	**35-39**
• **select and use** reference materials and resources as needed during the writing process.	**46, 194-196, 255-263, 264-268**
• **pay** attention to purpose and audience when developing writing.	**10, 40, 89, 101, 107, 129**
• **establish** a central idea (*topic sentence, focus, or thesis statement*), collect details, and organize supporting information for writing.	**47-48, 51**
• **use** anecdotes, descriptions, and vivid language to support the purpose of a written work.	**51-53, 83, 124-127, 153**
• **revise** selected drafts by adding, deleting, and rearranging copy—striving for better word choice and consistency.	**23, 55-59, 60-63, 84**
• **edit** drafts to ensure standard usage, varied sentence structure, appropriate word choice, capitalization, punctuation, correct spelling and format.	**64-67**
• **use** available technology to support aspects of creating, drafting, revising, editing, and publishing texts.	**24-29, 68-72, 269**

Evaluating Written Work

The student is expected to . . .   Handbook Pages

• **assess** writing according to the traits of effective writing.	**18-23, 55-59**
• **respond** in constructive ways to others' writing.	**60-63, 274**
• **use** published examples as models for writing.	**128**
• **review** a collection of his or her own writing to determine its strengths and weaknesses, and to set goals as a writer.	**30-33**

The Forms of Writing

Writing to Share

The student is expected to develop . . .   Handbook Pages

- **narratives** that . . .   **79, 138-143,**
  - recount in sequence several parts of a personal experience **209-215, 216-219,**
    or fictitious tale.   **220-225, 226-231**
  - are enriched with details, dialogue, and personal feelings.

- **expository compositions** that . . .   **78, 80,**
  - include supporting paragraphs with simple facts, details, and **88-93,**
    explanations.   **156-163,**
  - conclude with a detailed summary linked to the purpose of the **188-191,**
    composition.   **368-369**

- **persuasive letters or compositions** that . . .   **81, 94-99,**
  - state a clear position in support of a proposition or proposal. **164-165**
  - support the position with relevant evidence.
  - address reader concerns.

- **research reports** that . . .   **188-191,**
  - contain a beginning, a middle, and an ending.   **192-203**
  - establish a central idea/topic.
  - support the central idea or topic with facts, details, examples
    and explanations.

- **poems** that . . .   **239-249**
  - include figures of speech.
  - reflect attention to sound and arrangement of words.
  - reflect awareness of the power of language.

- **summaries of reading materials** that . . .   **185-187**
  - contain the material's main ideas and supporting information.
  - are arranged in a logical order.

- **responses to literature** that . . .   **166-171, 274**
  - demonstrate an understanding of a literary work.
  - include a summary that contains the main idea and the most
    significant details.
  - support judgments through references to the text and to
    personal knowledge.

- **business letters** that . . .   **177-181, 182-183**
  - consider audience, purpose, and context.
  - include all the parts of a letter.
  - have a correctly addressed envelope.

Writing to Learn

The student is expected to . . .   Handbook Pages

- **write to learn** in all subjects in the following ways: **133-137, 171,**
  - keeping dialogue journals   **185-187, 343,**
  - using learning logs   **353-355, 375**
  - writing response journals
  - making lists
  - summarizing what is heard or read
  - connecting knowledge within and across the disciplines
  - synthesizing information

The Mechanics of Writing

Research

The student is expected to . . .   Handbook Pages

- **organize** prior knowledge about a topic using a graphic   **45, 273,**
  organizer or some other prewriting strategy.   **333-336**

- **generate** questions to direct research.   **194-195**

- **use** various reference materials such as the dictionary,   **260-261,**
  encyclopedia, almanac, thesaurus, atlas, and on-line   **265, 268,**
  information as an aid to writing.   **290-292**

- **use** print and electronic sources to locate books   **255-263,**
  and articles.   **264-269**

- **understand** and use tables of contents, chapter and section   **262**
  headings, glossaries, indexes, and appendices to locate
  information in reference books.

- **take** notes from sources such as guest speakers, periodicals,   **196, 326, 331,**
  books, on-line sites, and so on.   **374-375**

- **summarize** and organize ideas gained from multiple   **46, 185-187,**
  sources.   **194-197**

- **evaluate** the research and frame new questions   **194, 268**
  for further investigation.

- **follow** accepted formats for writing research papers,   **201-203**
  including documenting sources.

- **give** credit for quotations and information in a bibliography   **196, 201, 203**
  (*works-cited page*).

Grammar and Usage

The student is expected to . . .   Handbook Pages

- **employ** standard English—including correct subject-verb agreement, pronoun-antecedent agreement, verb forms, and so on—to communicate clearly and effectively in writing.   **116-117, 305, 413, 421-424, 425-429**

- **understand** the different parts of speech.   **417-435**

- **write** in complete sentences (and eliminate sentence errors in writing).   **114-115, 412-416**

- **vary** the types of sentences in writing (*simple, compound, complex*).   **65, 118-121, 415-416**

- **use** conjunctions to connect ideas meaningfully.   **121, 380, 435**

- **make** writing precise and vivid using action verbs, specific nouns, and colorful modifiers.   **122-127**

- **learn** vocabulary-building strategies.   **288-305**

- **correctly use** commonly misused words.   **402-411**

Punctuation, Capitalization, and Spelling

The student is expected to . . .   Handbook Pages

- **use** correct punctuation and capitalization in writing.   **377-388, 389-392**

- **spell** accurately in final drafts, including frequently misspelled words, contractions, plurals, and homophones.   **306-309, 384-385, 394-395, 398-401, 402-411**

- **spell** derivatives correctly.   **294-304, 309**

- **use** syllable constructions and syllable boundary patterns to spell correctly.   **290-291**

- **understand** the influence of other languages and cultures on the spelling of English words.   **437-439**

Using *Writers Express* to Meet the Needs of Every Student

Teachers can't possibly accommodate all of their students' different learning styles following a standard text, one chapter after another. What works best is a language resource like *Writers Express*, providing useful information and guidelines that each student can turn to on his or her own terms.

Students refer to *Writers Express* when they need information—in any class, at any time. We like to call *Writers Express* a con-textbook because students use it, in context, as they develop a piece of writing, study for a test, prepare for an interview, and so on. *Writers Express,* more than a textbook can, evokes student-directed learning. It accommodates the different learning needs of all students.

1 Reform and Restructuring

We strongly believe that the primary role of instruction should be to help students improve their emerging learning abilities and explore their own interests. Instead of the assembly-line approach to teaching, with homogeneous students as the end product, students should be met on their own terms, with their individual needs at the core of the curriculum. For educators to do this, they must change their approach: Whether each learner is progressing must be the main concern, not the level of content covered.

2 Student-Centered Learning

Certainly this method of instruction makes the most sense in language arts instruction since no two students progress as writers and readers at the same speed or in the same way. To make instruction more student centered, many language arts teachers run their classrooms as writing and reading workshops. In workshops, students write at their own pace, read books that interest them, interact, take risks, decide what projects to work on next, and so on.

We've used the workshop approach in our own classrooms, so we know how effective it can be. Former students tell us all the time how they really learned to write and read in our language arts classes. It's also because of the workshop approach that we developed our first handbook. We did it to give our students a basic resource they could refer to when writing and learning.

3 Meeting Everyone's Needs

Once your students have their own copies of *Writers Express*, we can't urge you enough to turn your classroom into a workshop. It is the best way to meet your students' individual needs. Everyone reads, writes, and learns together. When workshops are used effectively, large-scale grouping or tracking isn't necessary.

4 Making It Work

Workshop teachers must become effective managers of their classrooms, providing an atmosphere conducive to writing and learning. They must guide students during personal conferences and editing sessions, and in occasional whole-class instruction, toward a mastery of basic skills.

Using the Handbook with the Complete *Writers Express* Program

The *Writers Express* handbook works by itself as an extremely effective writing and learning guide and can be used for a number of different purposes—many of which are discussed on the previous pages in this section of your *Teacher's Guide*.

The handbook also serves as the core resource for the ***Writers Express Language Program.*** There is a separate program of activities for each grade level—4 and 5. (See below for more information.)

Working with the Program

Students refer to the *Writers Express* handbook to help them complete their work in the program.

Teachers refer to the *Teacher's Guide* (this guide) for basic planning ideas, start-up activities, and mini-lessons.

Teachers who purchase the complete program receive a *Program Guide* ring binder for their grade level, providing teaching units for each chapter in the handbook (with daily lesson plans and blackline masters), editing and proofreading practice activities, and much more. All program guide activities are reproducible.

Special Note: The editing and proofreading practice activities are also available in a bound *SkillsBook* for each grade level.

The Process of Writing

Introductory Notes

This section introduces "The Process of Writing" chapters in the handbook and provides getting-started ideas to help you with your initial planning.

A Basic Writing Guide

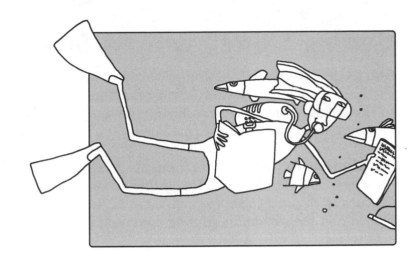

(See handbook pages 3-7.)

Children are filled with questions about their learning, just as teachers are about their teaching. This chapter answers some questions about writing and the places where these issues are addressed in the handbook. It guides the students to find different pages and sections of the handbook—places that will help them as they learn each day.

Rationale
- Students have many questions about writing that can be addressed.
- Students need straightforward answers to their questions to help them understand that the writing process need not be a mystery.

Major Concepts
- **Writing about topics they know about or have an interest in helps students become comfortable with the writing process.** (page 4)
- **The amount of prewriting students do depends on their knowledge of a subject.** (page 4)
- **Most writing needs a plan and a focus.** (page 5)
- **The writing process involves choosing what to put in a draft.** (page 5)
- **Students can learn to write with style.** (page 6)
- **Revising makes writing "as good as it can be."** (page 6)
- **Students should correct as many mistakes in grammar, mechanics, and usage as they can.** (page 7)
- **Students should learn to judge their own writing.** (page 7)

Performance Standards
Students are expected to . . .
- approach writing as a process to help them meet all of their writing challenges.
- assess writing according to certain standards.

Getting Started with "A Basic Writing Guide"

Start-Up Activity: Help students take some of the mystery out of writing by discussing the questions and answers in this chapter. If possible, relate the questions and answers to the written work students have already accomplished—for example, the work they have accumulated in their school portfolios.

Enrichment Activity: Invite students to share memories (good and not-so-good) of writing they have done in the past. If possible, have them bring some of their previous work to class. Discuss with your class the questions in this chapter, as they relate to this previous work. How did students handle finding a subject, getting started, and so on?

Teaching Resources

Writers Express Teacher's Guide

- Minilessons:
  Grades 4 and 5
  "A Writer's Question" (page 226)
- "The Process Approach" (pages 162-163)

Writers Express Handbook

- "One Writer's Process," pages 12-17, leads students through the steps one writer uses to develop a character sketch using the writing process.
- "Prewriting and Drafting," pages 34-53, and "Revising and Editing," pages 54-73, give guidelines for each step in the writing process.

Writers Express Program Guide

- A teaching unit (lesson plans and blackline masters) can be found in the Program Guide ring binder for each grade level.

Steps in the Writing Process/ One Writer's Process

(See handbook pages 8-11 and 12-17.)

While writing is done in a series of steps (prewriting, drafting, revising, and editing/proofreading), writers think, experiment, and review at each stage. As students learn to use the writing process, they become more confident and skilled writers.

Rationale
- Students should devote attention to generating ideas, planning their writing, drafting, and rewriting.
- Students who succeed in getting their thoughts down on paper feel more confident with future writing assignments and written tests.

Major Concepts
- **It takes time to learn the writing process.** (page 8)
- **Writing for others often involves prewriting, drafting, revising, editing, proofreading, and publishing.** (pages 9-11)
- **Prewriting involves choosing a subject and gathering details.** (page 13)
- **First drafts are often written freely.** (page 14)
- **Revising involves looking at overall completeness and clarity.** (page 15)
- **When editing and proofreading, writers look at every word.** (page 16)
- **Published writing should be correct and neatly designed.** (page 17)

Performance Standards

Students are expected to . . .
- approach writing as a process to help them meet their writing challenges.
- use prewriting strategies to collect, generate, and organize ideas.
- organize information with a graphic organizer or an outline.
- revise selected drafts by adding, deleting, and rearranging text.
- edit drafts to ensure accuracy in text and format.

Getting Started with "Steps in the Writing Process/One Writer's Process"

Start-Up Activity: Get permission from one or two of your students to use their papers as models for demonstrating the writing process in action. Make transparencies showing a first draft, some revision work, and editing/proofreading. Have the student(s) comment on his or her work, helping the others to experience, in reality, "one writer's process."

Enrichment Activity: As a review of the steps in the writing process, give students opportunities to discuss ways in which they have been successful or unsuccessful in using the writing process in the past. If possible, have them accompany this discussion with samples of writing from their portfolios or writing folders.

Teaching Resources

Writers Express Teacher's Guide

- Minilessons:

  Grade 4
  "Getting Started" (page 226)
  "Focus Pocus" (page 226)

  Grade 5
  "Why Five?" (page 226)
  "Be a writing detective." (page 227)

- "The Process Approach" (pages 162-163)

Writers Express Handbook

- "Steps in the Writing Process," pages 8-11, elaborates on each step the student writer in "One Writer's Process" uses to produce her finished piece.

- The writing process is further developed in "Prewriting and Drafting," pages 34-53, and "Revising and Editing," pages 54-73.

Writers Express Program Guide

- A teaching unit (lesson plans and blackline masters) can be found in the Program Guide ring binder for each grade level.

Traits of Effective Writing

(See handbook pages 18-23.)

Children can take specific steps to improve their writing. They start by learning the traits of sound writing. These traits include stimulating ideas, logical organization, engaging voice, original word choice, smooth-reading sentences, and correct, accurate copy.

Rationale

- Defining the traits of good writing, pointing them out in examples of literature, and asking students to consider these traits as they revise their work will acquaint young writers with the elements of good writing.
- Though some writers may be more talented than others, working with the traits can help all writers expand their skills.

Major Concepts

- **Effective writing is characterized by specific features, or traits, that can be identified and described.** (pages 18-19)
- **Good literature models key traits of effective writing.** (pages 20-22)
- **Students who understand these traits can use them to identify strengths or weaknesses in their own writing and in others' work.** (page 23)

Performance Standards - - - - -

Students are expected to . . .
- assess writing according to standards.
- analyze published examples as models for writing.
- review a collection of their own written works to determine its strengths and weaknesses.

Getting Started with "Traits of Effective Writing"

Start-Up Activity: The best way for students to learn about the traits of effective writing is to become aware of them in their reading. Read the examples of each trait on pages 20-22 in the handbook. Then, as students are doing their reading assignments, have them find additional examples for each of the traits. Periodically, have a time for sharing these reading excerpts.

Enrichment Activity: Perhaps the most difficult trait of effective writing for students to understand is personal voice. Try this activity to get the idea across: Select a passage from each of three books by authors the students are familiar with. Name the three authors; then read each passage aloud. Ask students to match the author to the passage.

Teaching Resources

Writers Express Teacher's Guide

- Minilessons:

  Grade 4
  "Very Effective!" (page 227)

  Grade 5
  "Even Better" (page 227)

- "The Trait-Based Approach" (pages 166-167)
- "Assessment Strategies and Rubrics" (pages 179-194)

Writers Express Handbook

- "Revising your Writing," pages 55-59, incorporates the traits of good writing into the revising process.

- "Checking for Word Choice," page 66, reinforces the traits of personal voice and original word choice.

Writers Express Program Guide

- A teaching unit (lesson plans and blackline masters) can be found in the Program Guide ring binder for each grade level.

Writing with Computers

(See handbook pages 24-29.)

Computer knowledge may be considered the "next step" in the writing process. Students with lots of computer experience can use it for all the steps—prewriting through publishing. Others may find it easier to take notes and make plans on paper. Then they can key in their writing and continue the process from there. Warning: Students need to learn that spell checkers cannot solve all spelling problems!

Rationale
- Computers are a part of modern life. Students should learn to use them as early as possible.
- Many students have access to computer labs, on-line computer services, and the Internet.

Major Concepts
- **Word-processing programs are important tools for writers.** (pages 24-25)
- **Writers can benefit from special tips when using computers.** (page 26)
- **Writing terms related to the computer include *character, font,* and *keyboard.* (page 27)

Performance Standards
Students are expected to . . .
- use available technology to support aspects of creating, revising, editing, and publishing texts.

Getting Started with "Writing with Computers"

Start-Up Activity: Discuss with students the significance of learning to keyboard—not only as it will affect their future school years, but quite possibly as it will impact their careers. There are many, many jobs in which experience with a computer will be necessary, not only in offices, but also in factories, automobile service facilities, retail stores, etc. Encourage students to become familiar with computers.

Enrichment Activity: If you have a computer to use, design a page that goes against the design rules listed on page 26 in the handbook. Put it on an overhead or pass it around the class. Ask for suggestions to improve the design.

Teaching Resources

Writers Express Teacher's Guide

- Minilessons:
  Grades 4 and 5
  "All Dressed Up" (page 227)

Writers Express Handbook

- "Computer Keyboard," pages 28-29, gives students a place to practice keyboarding and shows the proper placement of fingers on the keyboard.

- "Using the Internet," pages 264-269, presents more information on using computers in the classroom.

Writers Express Program Guide

- A teaching unit (lesson plans and blackline masters) can be found in the Program Guide ring binder for each grade level.

Planning Your Portfolio

(See handbook pages 30-33.)

A portfolio is a collection of written work or artwork. Two types of portfolios are mentioned in *Writers Express:* personal writing portfolios and classroom writing portfolios. The first is usually kept at home; the second is usually kept at school.

Rationale
- When students keep portfolios, they take charge of their own learning by reflecting on their work.
- Portfolios offer an alternative or a supplement to standardized testing.
- Portfolios require student reflection and choice. This kind of self-assessment can motivate personal learning.

Major Concepts
- **Each writer's personal portfolio says something about his or her talent and writing process.** (page 31)
- **A personal portfolio can include new ideas, important drafts, personal writing, and finished work.** (page 31)
- **Classroom portfolios can include a writer's best achievements or reflect his or her growth throughout the year.** (page 32)
- **Classroom portfolios differ from classroom writing folders.** (page 32)

Performance Standards

Students are expected to . . .
- review a collection of their work to determine strengths and weaknesses.

Getting Started with "Planning Your Portfolio"

Start-Up Activity: Explain to students that a writing portfolio, which each student will be keeping, is just one kind of portfolio. Many professionals—actors, models, artists, graphic designers, photographers, and financial managers—keep portfolios. Their portfolios include samples of their professional work and experiences.

Enrichment Activity: To encourage parents and guardians to support personal portfolios, your class could write them a friendly letter explaining the benefits of, and offering tips for making, a portfolio for creative work done at home, in church schools, in Scout groups, in 4-H, and so on. Periodically, students could bring these personal portfolios to school to share with their classmates.

Teaching Resources

Writers Express Teacher's Guide

- Minilessons:
  Grades 4 and 5
  "A Few Favorites" (page 227)
- "Assessment Strategies and Rubrics" (pages 179-194)

Writers Express Handbook

- "Publishing Tips," page 69, provides students with more help in preparing writing for a portfolio.

Writers Express Program Guide

- A teaching unit (lesson plans and blackline masters) can be found in the Program Guide ring binder for each grade level.

Choosing a Subject

(See handbook pages 35-39.)

Most writers have had the experience of new and surprising thoughts occurring to them as they write. It is just as true, however, that most writers make careful plans, keep lists of ideas, clip excerpts of great writing, and so on. In other words, writers engage in many behind-the-scenes activities before they sit down to write their first drafts.

Rationale	• Students need to develop strategies for identifying and choosing appropriate writing subjects.
	• Many writers jot down their ideas in a notebook or journal.
	• Writers usually write about things they know a lot about.

Major Concepts

- **Students are surrounded by ideas for writing.** (pages 36-37)
- **Using strategies to discover subjects makes prewriting easier.** (pages 36-37)
- **Prompts, quotations, and general topics can help students discover writing subjects.** (pages 38-39)

Performance Standards - - - - -

Students are expected to . . .

- use prewriting strategies such as brainstorming, freewriting, graphic organizers (clusters and webs), lists, notes, and logs to collect, generate, and organize ideas.
- select and use reference materials and resources as needed during the writing process.

Getting Started with "Choosing a Subject"

Start-Up Activity: Direct students to keep a section of their notebooks or journals for writing ideas. Suggest that they think and act like writers when they do this. They might divide their pages in sections like the following: new discoveries, ideas from books, wild ideas, important beliefs, and so on.

Enrichment Activity: Ask students to keep a life list of writing ideas. It could be an "I'll always remember" list, including names of people, animals, places, books and movies, important celebrations, blunders, and prized possessions. Students can add to this list whenever they'd like. They can also tap into it whenever they need a writing idea.

Teaching Resources

Writers Express Teacher's Guide

- Minilessons:

  Grade 4
  "Life Map" (page 228)

  Grade 5
  "Dust off your cluster, buster." (page 228)

Writers Express Handbook

- "Gathering Details and Making a Plan," pages 44-49, continues the discussion on prewriting activities.

Writers Express Program Guide

- A teaching unit (lesson plans and blackline masters) can be found in the Program Guide ring binder for each grade level.

Finding a Form

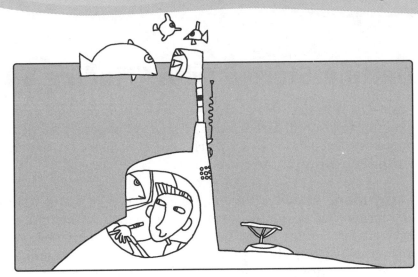

(See handbook pages 40-43.)

Each piece of writing takes a certain form: letter, report, poem, essay, etc. Understanding the proper use of a form is almost as important as knowing about the subject one is writing about. Some forms, such as essays and reports, require outside research. Other forms, including personal narratives and thank-you notes, spring from the writer's store of memories and ideas.

Rationale
- Writing takes many different forms, both formal and informal.
- Knowing about different forms of writing helps writers write.
- A writer can learn a lot about writing by experimenting with different forms.

Major Concepts
- **Finding the right form of writing is just as important as choosing the subject.** (page 40)
- **Writers can choose the type of writing (narrative, expository, descriptive, and persuasive) that suits their subject and then find an appropriate form.** (pages 41-42)
- **Writing-to-learn activities include learning logs, graphic organizers, notes, etc.** (page 42)

Performance Standards

Students are expected to . . .
- choose the appropriate form for their own writing, including journals, letters, poems, and narratives.
- pay careful attention to purpose and audience as they develop their writing.

Getting Started with "Finding a Form"

Start-Up Activity: Have students look through some of the books in your classroom to find examples of the different forms listed on pages 41-42 in the handbook. Place the headings *narrative, expository, descriptive,* and *persuasive* on the chalkboard, and have the students write their titles in the correct list.

Enrichment Activity: Students can learn a lot about writing by experimenting with different forms. For example, by writing travelogues, they are practicing descriptive writing, and by writing recipes, they are experimenting with how-to writing. Share examples of and discuss with the class some cartoon strips and e-mail messages. Under which types of writing (narrative, persuasive, etc.) can these forms fit?

Teaching Resources

Writers Express Teacher's Guide

- Minilessons:
  Grades 4 and 5
  "The Shape of Things to Come" (page 228)

Writers Express Handbook

- "Publishing Your Writing," pages 68-73, lists places that publish different forms of writing.

- "The Forms of Writing" section, pages 132-253, provides guidelines for many of the forms listed in this chapter.

Writers Express Program Guide

- A teaching unit (lesson plans and blackline masters) can be found in the Program Guide ring binder for each grade level.

Gathering Details and Making a Plan

(See handbook pages 44-49.)

During prewriting, students must gather details about their subjects. Interviewing and researching can help them do this. Before writing a first draft, students must also narrow their subjects (focus) and organize their details.

Rationale
- Students can use different strategies to gather details.
- Finding the focus helps the writer pay attention to the most important or interesting part of a subject.
- Students need to gather information and plan their work before they begin writing.

Major Concepts
- **After writers choose a subject, they need to identify what they already know about it and then gather more information.** (pages 44-45)
- **Students can gather information from interviews, books, and other reference works.** (page 46)
- **Writers stay organized when they find a focus and make a plan.** (page 47)
- **Use of graphic organizers, including outlines, helps students to organize their writing.** (pages 48-49)

Performance Standards

Students are expected to . . .
- use prewriting strategies such as brainstorming, freewriting, graphic organizers, lists, notes, and logs to collect, generate, and organize ideas.
- establish a central idea (topic sentence, focus, or thesis statement), collect details, and organize supporting information for writing.

Getting Started with "Gathering Details and Making a Plan"

Start-Up Activity: Give students choices when it comes to gathering information for writing projects. The list of ideas on page 45 in the handbook includes strategies as simple as *listing* and as colorful as *crazy questions.* Let students try different ones at different times.

Enrichment Activity: Organizing information for writing can be a big challenge and may be one of the most neglected tasks in writing. Help students to use the graphic organizers on pages 48-49 in the handbook, showing them how various organizers fit certain writing types especially well. These two statements conflict: each organizer coordinates to a specific type of writing, but a cluster and an outline can serve the same purpose.

Teaching Resources

Writers Express Teacher's Guide

- Minilessons:

  Grade 4
  "Pencil Talk" (page 228)

  Grade 5
  "Converse" (page 228)

Writers Express Handbook

- "Choosing a Subject," pages 35-39, acts as a lead-in to this chapter.

- "Using Reading Strategies," pages 271-279, shows several important graphic organizers.

Writers Express Program Guide

- A teaching unit (lesson plans and blackline masters) can be found in the Program Guide ring binder for each grade level.

Writing a First Draft

(See handbook pages 50-53.)

In school, there has always been a tendency to emphasize the product of writing—how it looks and how quickly it is finished. But children need to learn that good writing is more than completing a first draft. Learning about the steps in the writing process can put children at ease about their writing. Knowing the process assures them that taking time with their writing, sticking with it until it is something they are proud of, is the right thing to do.

Rationale

- Inexperienced writers often try to produce a finished piece in one sitting.
- During the first draft, writers should get their ideas on paper rather than be concerned with the fine points of grammar and mechanics. (They will address grammar and mechanics during the revising, editing, and proofreading steps.)

Major Concepts

- **The first draft doesn't have to be perfect.** (page 50)
- **There are a variety of ways to begin a first draft.** (page 51)
- **The middle part of a draft should share or explain the main points of a subject.** (page 52)
- **The ending of a draft should give the reader a sense of satisfaction about the subject.** (page 53)

Performance Standards

Students are expected to . . .
- structure drafts that include several connected sentences or paragraphs on the same topic.
- focus on a central idea.
- use anecdotes, descriptions, and vivid language to support the purpose of a written work.

Getting Started with "Writing a First Draft"

Start-Up Activity: To demonstrate the writing process, write the first draft of a letter or memo to the students' parents, with input from the class. (Use an overhead transparency or the chalkboard.) After you revise the letter or memo, show students how much or how little of the first draft remains. This shows students the writing process in action.

Enrichment Activity: As often as possible, model and share your own writing with your class. If you do not feel you are a strong writer, try to write at least once a day—for example, write in a journal when your students are doing the same.

Teaching Resources

Writers Express Teacher's Guide

- Minilessons:

  Grade 4
  "Sentence Factory" (page 229)

  Grade 5
  "Tell me more." (page 229)

Writers Express Handbook

- "Gathering Details and Making a Plan," pages 44-49, helps students find a focus for their first drafts and organize their supporting details.

- "Putting Things in Order," page 84, shows three ways to effectively organize details in a first draft.

Writers Express Program Guide

- A teaching unit (lesson plans and blackline masters) can be found in the Program Guide ring binder for each grade level.

Revising Your Writing/ Revising with Partners

(See handbook pages 55-63.)

Writers improve their work by reading it over and rewriting the sections that need help. This process is called revision, checking for meaning, voice, and clarity. Students can benefit by revising with a partner, and clear guidelines for these conferences will ensure their success.

Rationale

- Many students think that good writers sit down and write finished, polished pieces the first time through. This rarely happens.
- Many students are uncomfortable with revision because they fear their ideas will be changed. Information about revision leads to new understandings about writing.
- When writers read their work to others and get a response, they begin to understand the strengths and weaknesses of their writing.

Major Concepts

- **Writing can be changed before it's published—unlike spoken conversations—so that it more closely reflects what the writer means.** (page 55)
- **Writers need to look for both strong and weak parts in their work.** (page 56)
- **Writers benefit from the use of revision checklists.** (pages 57, 63)
- **Writers can follow specific tips to improve their work.** (pages 58-59)
- **Revision is easier when writers work with partners.** (pages 60-62)

Performance Standards

Students are expected to . . .
- revise selected drafts by adding, deleting, and rearranging text, striving for better word choice and consistency.
- respond in constructive ways to others' writing.

Getting Started with "Revising Your Writing/ Revising with Partners"

Start-Up Activity: Students' revising time should be active, but as quiet as possible. You might designate a quiet place in the middle of the room, and assign other areas as places for discussion. Be sure the students know how to make an "appointment" for a conference with you.

Enrichment Activity: Hold writing conferences with your students. Group conferences work well for students who have a similar need, or when the writer needs lots of feedback. A paired conference works well for editing and proofreading, or when a student is reluctant to read his or her work to a larger group. Teacher conferences work well when they are requested by a student, or when the teacher sets up a schedule of conferences for specific writers and needs. (This can be done very simply by writing the invitation "Conference Times" on the chalkboard.)

Teaching Resources

Writers Express Teacher's Guide

- Minilessons:

  Grades 4 and 5
  "Before and After" (page 229)
  "Saying the Right Thing" (page 229)

Writers Express Handbook

- "Traits of Effective Writing," pages 18-23, covers helpful revising information.

- "Putting Things in Order," page 84, shows three ways to effectively organize details in a first draft.

Writers Express Program Guide

- A teaching unit (lesson plans and blackline masters) can be found in the Program Guide ring binder for each grade level.

Editing and Proofreading

(See handbook pages 64-67.)

When writing and revising first drafts, students strive to present creative ideas clearly and completely. Next, they must edit and proofread their work. During those steps, they can smooth out the inevitable bumps in sentence structure and eliminate errors in mechanics and usage.

Rationale

- Published (shared) writing that contains errors may not be taken seriously. Therefore, students must know how to edit and proofread their writing.
- Students who have worked to write and revise their writing also need to edit and proofread their writing.
- Students can take pride in neat, correct final drafts of their work.

Major Concepts

- **Editing and proofreading entails polishing your writing—getting rid of careless errors and making every word count.** (page 64)
- **While editing, students should make sure that their sentences read smoothly.** (page 65)
- **Another important editing task is choosing the right words. This involves using powerful words as well as avoiding usage errors.** (page 66)
- **An editing and proofreading checklist is a useful tool, reminding students to use proper punctuation, capitalization, and spelling.** (page 67)

Performance Standards

Students are expected to . . .
- edit drafts to ensure standard usage, varied sentence structure, appropriate word choice, correct spelling, capitalization, punctuation, and format.
- assess writing according to standards.

Getting Started with "Editing and Proofreading"

Start-Up Activity: By the time students get to the editing and proofreading stage of their writing, they may be hesitant to make more changes. Encourage and assist them in understanding what it means to check for smooth sentences, word choice, and so on. Reading and discussing pages 65 and 66 in the handbook could be helpful. Be sure to give students plenty of time to do their editing and proofreading.

Enrichment Activity: Early in the year, limit students' responsibility for editing and proofreading to two or three major skills—for example, you might have them look especially for sentence capitalization and end punctuation plus spelling of high-frequency words. Then, throughout the year, gradually give instruction and add other skills.

Teaching Resources

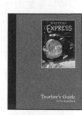

Writers Express Teacher's Guide

- Minilessons:

  Grades 4 and 5
  "Check!" (page 230)

Writers Express Handbook

- The "Proofreader's Guide," pages 377-435, has specific information about punctuation, capitalization, usage, and grammar.

Writers Express Program Guide

- A teaching unit (lesson plans and blackline masters) can be found in the Program Guide ring binder for each grade level.

Publishing Your Writing

(See handbook pages 68-73.)

Kent Brown, the publisher of *Highlights for Children,* knows that publishing is very powerful stuff. He doesn't remember too much about his fourth-grade class, but he does recall the day his teacher hung his Thanksgiving turkey on the wall. He felt proud when she commented on how good it was. Children may not remember everything they write, but they remember the things they publish.

Rationale
- Published work is special work. Seeing one's own work published helps build self-esteem.
- By reading other students' work (fiction and nonfiction), young people begin to discover how others in their class view their world.
- Published writers want to write more, and they tend to read more.

Major Concepts
- **Publishing makes writing worth the effort.** (page 68)
- **Preparing a piece of writing for publishing takes special time and effort.** (page 69)
- **There are many ways to publish writing.** (pages 70-72)
- **Sometimes writing can be bound into a book.** (page 73)

Performance Standards

Students are expected to . . .
- share finished pieces with classmates and others.

Getting Started with "Publishing Your Writing"

Start-Up Activity: Suggest that small groups of students publish a group poetry sheet. First appoint the groups, and then let them choose a theme for their poetry. They may choose the poetry form from pages 246-249 in the handbook. After each member writes a poem and refines it, the groups must decide how to publish their poems. Encourage them to use the publishing suggestions on pages 70-73 in the handbook.

Enrichment Activity: Consider having the fifth edition of the *Market Guide for Young Writers: Where and How to Sell What You Write* by Kathy Henderson (Writers Digest Books, 1996) available in your classroom or school library. It lists many magazines where students can submit writing.

Teaching Resources

Writers Express Teacher's Guide

- Minilessons:
  Grades 4 and 5
  "It's personal." (page 230)

Writers Express Handbook

- "The Forms of Writing," pages 132-253, gives guidelines for many forms of writing that could be published.
- The "Proofreader's Guide," pages 377-435, has specific information about punctuation, capitalization, usage, and grammar.

Writers Express Program Guide

- A teaching unit (lesson plans and blackline masters) can be found in the Program Guide ring binder for each grade level.

Writing Paragraphs

(See handbook pages 75-87.)

A paragraph is a group of sentences focusing on one specific topic. Students can develop paragraphs as stories, descriptions, explanations, or opinions. The type of paragraph depends upon the topic, the kinds of details the writer is able to gather, and the audience. A paragraph must contain enough details to give the reader a complete picture of the topic.

Rationale

- Paragraphs are the building blocks of stories, essays, and articles.
- Sentences within paragraphs, and paragraphs within longer texts, require linking words and transitions.
- Paragraphs help readers make sense of longer pieces of writing, so learning to write and identify paragraphs is important.

Major Concepts

- **A paragraph is a group of sentences that tells about one idea.** (page 75)
- **Paragraphs have three basic parts: the topic sentence, the body, and the closing sentence.** (pages 76-77)
- **There are four different types of paragraphs.** (pages 78-81)
- **Planning is an important step in writing paragraphs.** (page 82)
- **Supporting details in paragraphs come from various sources.** (page 83)
- **Paragraphs can be organized in different ways.** (page 84)
- **Transition words "glue" sentences in paragraphs together.** (page 85)

Performance Standards

Students are expected to write paragraphs that . . .
- contain three or more sentences about the same subject.
- develop a topic sentence.
- include simple supporting facts and descriptive details.
- include a closing sentence that reminds readers of what the paragraph is about.
- are held together with transitions.

Getting Started with "Writing Paragraphs"

Start-Up Activity: Using the guidelines on page 82 in the handbook, model paragraph writing with your students. First choose a subject and discuss the paragraph's purpose, audience, and form. Then gather information. Next put your paragraph in order by writing a topic sentence, the body, and the closing sentence. Finally, demonstrate how you revise your work.

Enrichment Activity: Some students have difficulty finding paragraphs in their own writing because they haven't ordered their sentences well. Find a sample of such a paper (with permission from the student writer). As a class activity, work on reordering the sentences. Then use the three-step process on pages 86-87 in the handbook to find the paragraphs in the paper.

Teaching Resources

Writers Express Teacher's Guide

- Minilessons:

  Grade 4
  "Twins" (page 230)

  Grade 5
  "Details, Details" (page 230)

- "Assessment Strategies and Rubrics" (pages 179-194)

Writers Express Handbook

- "Thinking and Writing," pages 338-345, contains additional sample paragraphs based on different kinds of thinking.

Writers Express Program Guide

- A teaching unit (lesson plans and blackline masters) can be found in the Program Guide ring binder for each grade level.

Writing Expository Essays

(See handbook pages 88-93.)

When students write expository essays, they demonstrate their knowledge of a subject or their ability to explain something. Writing expository essays can serve as a learning ground for taking essay exams in years to come.

Rationale
- Writing expository essays can help students clarify their thinking about a subject.
- Expository writing skills enable students to share their knowledge.
- Students will use expository writing throughout their school years and beyond.

Major Concepts
- **The purpose of an expository essay is to inform.** (page 88)
- **Writing an essay involves the same steps used to write a paragraph.** (pages 89-90)
- **Each part of an essay—beginning, middle, and ending—has an important purpose.** (pages 90-91)
- **Many expository essays are organized according to the comparison and contrast method.** (pages 92-93)

Performance Standards

Students are expected to . . .
- write expository compositions that include supporting paragraphs with facts, details, and explanations.
- conclude expository compositions with a summary linked to the main idea.

Getting Started with "Writing Expository Essays"

Start-Up Activity: Share an essay from a news magazine written for children. Following the reading, help students identify the subject and focus, as well as the voice and audience of the essay. (Use handbook page 89 with this activity.) Post this information so students can refer to it when they are writing their essays.

Enrichment Activity: Read an expository essay you've selected (from a magazine, newspaper, book, etc.) to the class. Using the revising and editing questions on page 90 in *Writers Express*, review the essay with students.

Teaching Resources

Writers Express Teacher's Guide

- Minilessons:
  Grade 4
  "Read all about it." (page 230)
  Grade 5
  "What's the big idea?" (page 231)
- "Assessment Strategies and Rubrics" (page 183 and 185)

Writers Express Handbook

- "Develop a Writing Plan," page 47, leads students in developing a focus, or thesis statement.
- "Writing a First Draft," pages 50-53, gives students tips on developing the beginning, middle, and ending for their essays.
- "How-To Writing," pages 172-175, provides five additional sample expository essays.

Writers Express Program Guide

- A teaching unit (lesson plans and blackline masters) can be found in the Program Guide ring binder for each grade level.

Writing Persuasive Essays

(See handbook pages 94-99.)

When students write persuasive essays, they have to be sure enough about their topic to be convincing. They must understand the difference between opinion and fact and know how to combine the two to sway readers.

Rationale
- Everyone has opinions, and most people like to share them.
- Writing persuasive essays helps students learn how to form opinions based on facts.
- Students need to learn how to support their opinions.
- Students must learn how to address opposing opinions.

Major Concepts
- **A persuasive essay supports an opinion.** (page 94)
- **The subject of a persuasive essay should be specific and appropriate for the audience.** (page 95)
- **Each part of an essay—beginning, middle, and ending—has an important purpose.** (page 97)
- **Most persuasive essays use facts to support an opinion.** (page 98)
- **Some persuasive essays use humor to make a point.** (page 99)

Performance Standards

Students are expected to . . .
- develop a clear position in support of a proposition or proposal.
- support a position with relevant evidence.
- address readers' concerns.

Getting Started with "Writing Persuasive Essays"

Start-Up Activity: Is there a controversy at your school? In the community? Introduce some details of a current controversy to give students a little background. Then ask for volunteers to debate each side of the subject. You might have the students compose essays on each side of the controversy.

Enrichment Activity: Editorial pages of a newspaper are a fabulous source of persuasive writing. As a class, analyze a few editorials or letters to the editor. Point out the different ways writers support their opinions. Discuss the editorials that seem most believable and try to analyze why that is so.

Teaching Resources

Writers Express Teacher's Guide

- Minilessons:
  Grade 4
  "We need a night off!" (page 231)
  Grade 5
  "Very Funny" (page 231)
- "Assessment Strategies and Rubrics" (pages 183 and 186)

Writers Express Handbook

- "Writing a Letter to the Editor," pages 164-165, provides tips and a sample letter to the editor, another type of persuasive writing.

- "Thinking Clearly," pages 346-351, helps students differentiate between fact and opinion as well as recognize "fuzzy thinking."

Writers Express Program Guide

- A teaching unit (lesson plans and blackline masters) can be found in the Program Guide ring binder for each grade level.

Descriptive Writing

(See handbook pages 100-105.)

Good writers describe things well. They use words related to the five senses and compare their subjects to other familiar things. When readers sit down with a piece of good writing, they can picture the people, places, objects, or ideas that the writer is describing.

Rationale
- Young writers must learn to pay attention to detail.
- The world is full of people, places, and things to describe.
- If writers can describe something or someone clearly, they have an understanding of that subject.

Major Concepts
- **Descriptive writing makes a subject come alive for an audience.** (pages 100-101)
- **Descriptive writing uses many kinds of details.** (pages 100-105)
- **A descriptive essay can describe a person, a place, or an object.** (pages 103-105)

Performance Standards

Students are expected to . . .
- use anecdotes, descriptions, and vivid language to support the purpose of a written work.

Getting Started with "Descriptive Writing"

Start-Up Activity: Describe one of the students without revealing his or her name. See if anyone can tell who it is from your description. Then ask for volunteers to do the same. When you are finished with this activity, reflect on the language used in the oral descriptions. Encourage students to use similar details when they are writing descriptions.

Enrichment Activity: Bring to class something that has a strange shape, texture, or consistency (examples: starfish, tree bark, cooked spaghetti). Arrange it so that students may touch, smell, and taste (if this is appropriate) the object, but not see it. Have them use as many descriptive words as they can to define the object.

Teaching Resources

Writers Express Teacher's Guide

- Minilessons:

  Grade 4
  "White Whiskers Twitch" (page 231)

  Grade 5
  "Bouncing Basketballs" (page 232)

Writers Express Handbook

- "Sample Descriptive Paragraph," page 78, gives students another model to learn from.

Writers Express Program Guide

- A teaching unit (lesson plans and blackline masters) can be found in the Program Guide ring binder for each grade level.

Narrative Writing

(See handbook pages 106-111.)

Most people love to tell stories about themselves or others and do so with a natural ease. They can also learn to write their stories down. Although writing requires more work, it makes the stories available to a larger audience.

Rationale
- Writing narratives puts students in touch with their world.
- Telling and writing stories is an ancient practice.

Major Concepts
- **Writing stories differs from telling them.** (page 106)
- **Answering the 5 W's can help students plan their narratives.** (page 107)
- **Some narratives are based on personal memories and events.** (pages 109-110)
- **Using a writing-and-revising checklist encourages good story writing.** (page 111)

Performance Standards

Students are expected to . . .
- recount in sequence several parts of a personal experience or fictitious tale.
- establish characters, a problem, and a setting.

Getting Started with "Narrative Writing"

Start-Up Activity: Using the words "I'll never forget the time . . . ," have students make a list of memories that complete that phrase. From their list, invite them to tell at least one story. Explain that stories like these can be the basis for writing narratives.

Enrichment Activity: Memories are powerful writing subjects for personal narratives, and for songs, TV shows, and movies, as well. Ask students to recall and listen for songs, shows, or movies that are based on memories.

Teaching Resources

Writers Express Teacher's Guide

- Minilessons:

  Grade 4
  "Remember and Remember" (page 232)

  Grade 5
  "That's a different story." (page 232)

- "Assessment Strategies and Rubrics" (pages 183 and 184)

Writers Express Handbook

- "Sample Narrative Paragraph," page 79, provides hints for including details in narrative writing.

- "Writing Personal Narratives," pages 138-143, offers students an expanded, more focused type of narrative to develop.

Writers Express Program Guide

- A teaching unit (lesson plans and blackline masters) can be found in the Program Guide ring binder for each grade level.

Writing Basic Sentences

(See handbook pages 113-117.)

As students edit their writing, they should review their sentences—checking that each sentence expresses a clear and complete thought and fits in with the rest of the piece. Suggest that students refer to this chapter whenever they edit.

Rationale

- It is important for students to fine-tune their sentence sense, to know what is and what isn't a sentence.
- Students need to know what to look for when they edit their sentences.
- Students need to take pride in their writing, striving to express their ideas clearly and effectively.

Major Concepts

- **All sentences have a subject and a verb. The subjects and verbs must agree.** (pages 114, 116)
- **Checking for sentence errors is an important editing task.** (pages 115-117)
- **Common sentence errors include sentence fragments, run-on sentences, and rambling sentences.** (page 115)
- **Sentences should be checked for double subjects, pronoun-antecedent agreement, and double negatives.** (page 117)

Performance Standards

Students are expected to . . .
- employ standard English grammar and usage to communicate clearly and effectively.
- write in complete sentences, varying the length and types.
- eliminate sentence fragments, run-on sentences, and rambling sentences.

Getting Started with "Writing Basic Sentences"

Start-Up Activity: Provide students with several pairings of a subject and verb. (Examples: Dogs chase. Cats scramble.) Have them add words that describe or complete the thought to make an interesting, accurate sentence. Then have them create compound subjects in their sentences by adding one or more nouns connected with *and* or *or.* Check all sentences for subject-verb agreement.

Enrichment Activity: Have students write a rambling sentence about how they spent one day. It could be a day at school, at an amusement park, or anywhere. When they are done, have them exchange papers and correct each other's sentence.

Teaching Resources

Writers Express Teacher's Guide

- Minilessons:
  Grade 4
  "Running into . . ." (page 232)
  Grade 5
  "And so on, and so on . . ." (page 233)

Writers Express Handbook

- "Combining Sentences," pages 118-121, takes students to the next level of writing sentences.
- "Writing with Style," pages 122-131, provides tips on choosing words and developing a writing voice.
- "Understanding Sentences," pages 412-416, defines basic sentence parts and how they work together.

Writers Express Program Guide

- A teaching unit (lesson plans and blackline masters) can be found in the Program Guide ring binder for each grade level.

Combining Sentences

(See handbook pages 118-121.)

Learning to combine short, simple sentences into more complex ones improves writing quality, especially in terms of syntactic proficiency. The ability to combine sentences is very helpful during revising and editing when students focus on sentence structure.

Rationale

- Sentence combining promotes greater skill in writing sentences.
- Sentence combining helps students become attentive to their writing.
- Sentence combining encourages appreciation of the language.

Major Concepts

- **Ideas from short sentences can be combined by moving a key word from one sentence to the other.** (page 119)
- **Ideas from short sentences can be combined into one sentence using a series of words or phrases.** (page 119)
- **Ideas from short sentences can be combined into one sentence using a phrase.** (page 120)
- **Two sentences can be combined using compound subjects or verbs.** (page 120)
- **Two or more simple sentences can be combined into a compound sentence.** (page 121)
- **Two or more ideas can be combined into a complex sentence.** (page 121)

Performance Standards

Students are expected to . . .
- write in complete sentences, varying the sentence lengths and types.
- develop an awareness of compound and complex sentences.
- use conjunctions to connect dependent and independent clauses.

Getting Started with "Combining Sentences"

Start-Up Activity: Read the introduction to sentence combining on page 118. Using a current topic of study, have each student write five short sentences about the topic. Then ask the students to work with a partner to combine short sentences into longer ones.

Enrichment Activity: Have students choose a current writing assignment and check it for short sentences that could be combined into longer sentences.

Teaching Resources

Writers Express Teacher's Guide

- Minilessons:

  Grade 4
  "Combo Challenge" (page 233)

  Grade 5
  "Make it flow, bro." (page 233)

Writers Express Handbook

- "Checking for Smooth Sentences," page 65, advises students to vary sentence structure and watch for sentence errors.

- "Types of Sentences," page 415, describes and models simple, compound, and complex sentences.

Writers Express Program Guide

- A teaching unit (lesson plans and blackline masters) can be found in the Program Guide ring binder for each grade level.

Writing with Style

(See handbook pages 122-131.)

Style varies from writer to writer, and it evolves as an author gains experience. Writers develop style; they aren't just born with it. Even young writers can develop and improve their style by studying and imitating the polished writing of their favorite authors.

Rationale
- Style is personal; it develops naturally as writers practice and gain experience.
- Writers can help develop their style by reading avidly, by writing regularly, and by modeling interesting sentences and passages.

Major Concepts
- **Young writers can develop a style that is "strong and healthy" if they follow specific guidelines.** (page 123)
- **Writing techniques are specific ways to improve style.** (pages 124-127)
- **Writers can learn from their favorite authors.** (page 128)
- **Writers use specific terms when talking about their writing.** (pages 129-131)

Performance Standards

Students are expected to . . .
- select vocabulary and voice with an awareness of audience and purpose.
- use anecdotes and descriptions with vivid, precise language to support the purpose of a written work.

Getting Started with "Writing with Style"

Start-Up Activity: Choose five of the writing techniques from pages 124-127. List them on the chalkboard for students to copy onto paper or a note card. Have students keep this list with them when they are reading a novel or a story in a reader. Then, when they spot one of these techniques, they should mark the page with a slip of paper and the name of the technique. After a few days, ask students to share their discoveries.

Enrichment Activity: Share an anecdote (brief story) to demonstrate a point you would like your students to remember. Explain that anecdotes can be included in writing when the writer wants to make a point. Read the anecdote on page 124 in the handbook. Discuss how, and where, this anecdote could be included in a story.

Teaching Resources

Writers Express Teacher's Guide

- Minilessons:

  Grade 4
  "You've got to please yourself." (page 233)

  Grade 5
  "Coming to Terms" (page 234)

Writers Express Handbook

- "Traits of Effective Writing," pages 18-23, introduces qualities contributing to writing style.

- "Checking for Smooth Sentences," page 65, advises students to vary sentence structure and watch for sentence errors.

- "Combining Sentences," pages 118-121, shows students how to create interesting sentences.

Writers Express Program Guide

- A teaching unit (lesson plans and blackline masters) can be found in the Program Guide ring binder for each grade level.

The Forms of Writing

Introductory Notes

This section introduces "The Forms of Writing" chapters in the handbook and provides getting-started ideas to help you with your initial planning.

Writing in Journals

(See handbook pages 133-137.)

A journal can be a notebook with blank pages or a simple, stapled stack of paper. In journals, students write to learn by making observations, capturing memories, and responding to literature. They also question, synthesize, and reflect upon their school learning and other life experiences.

Rationale

- Students learn by writing as they reflect on and process what they know and as they discover what they need to find out.
- As students write regularly in journals, their writing becomes more fluent.
- When seeking topics for writing, students can draw from their journal-recorded experiences.

Major Concepts

- **Students can use their journals to take notes, collect ideas for stories and poems, work out their feelings, and for many other reasons.** (pages 133-134)
- **It's important to have ways to get started and ways to keep going in journal writing.** (pages 134-135)
- **Journal writing can be done in a variety of formats and for a variety of reasons.** (page 136)

Performance Standards

Students are expected to . . .
- write to express, discover, record, develop, reflect on ideas, and solve problems.
- use writing (such as dialogue journals and learning logs) and techniques (such as making lists and summarizing) as tools for learning in all subjects.

Getting Started with "Writing in Journals"

Start-Up Activity: To encourage meaningful writing in journals, give your students something to ponder as they come into the classroom. For example, as a part of your classroom routine, pose a question related to something you are studying or a topic of current interest.

Enrichment Activity: Encourage students to look to their other school subjects (math, science, social studies, etc.) for material to reflect upon in their journals. Examples: What if the sun shone only one week per year? (Science) List as many reasons as you can for using maps. (Social Studies) What do you like about your favorite author's writing? (Reading)

Teaching Resources

Writers Express Teacher's Guide

- Minilessons:

  Grade 4
  "A Very Bad-Good Day" (page 235)

  Grade 5
  "I know just how she felt." (page 235)

Writers Express Handbook

- "Writing Prompts," page 38, lists topic ideas for journal writing.

- "Writing in a Response Journal," page 171, explains how journal writing can help students interact with their assigned or pleasure reading.

- "Writing as a Learning Tool," pages 353-355, shows students another use for journal writing.

Writers Express Program Guide

- A teaching unit (lesson plans and blackline masters) can be found in the Program Guide ring binder for each grade level.

Writing Personal Narratives

(See handbook pages 138-143.)

The best stories come from our most important, most significant memories. When students think back on their experiences and recall related details, they glean material for a personal narrative.

Rationale
- Writing personal narratives puts students in touch with themselves and with the world in which they live.
- Personal-narrative writing, with its ready supply of subject matter, is often an excellent starting point for reluctant writers.

Major Concepts
- **A personal narrative is a story about a personal memory.** (page 138)
- **Students can gather ideas by recalling specific events in their lives. It helps to keep track of some of these memories in a daily diary or journal.** (pages 140)
- **Students can follow specific steps in order to produce a satisfactory personal narrative.** (pages 141-142)
- **A family story is a very special kind of personal narrative.** (page 143)

Performance Standards

Students are expected to . . .
- recount in sequence several parts of a personal experience.
- create narratives that are enriched with details, dialogue, and personal feelings.
- revise drafts by adding, deleting, and rearranging text, striving for better word choice and consistency.
- use anecdotes, descriptions, and vivid language to support the purpose of a written work.

Getting Started with "Writing Personal Narratives"

Start-Up Activity: One way to get a class started with personal narratives is to share a story about an item that is special—a meaningful reason for having "show and tell." Invite students to bring in something that has a story attached to it. They could bring things like maps, postcards, toys, photographs, or special foods. (If students can't bring items in, they can still describe the items and tell their stories.)

Enrichment Activity: Have students write family stories—in particular, "Holiday Stories" and "Heirloom Stories." You can find specific directions for these on handbook page 143.

Teaching Resources

Writers Express Teacher's Guide

- Minilessons:

  Grade 4
  "Who am I?" (page 235)

  Grade 5
  "Listen, my friend." (page 235)

- "Assessment Strategies and Rubrics" (pages 183-184)

Writers Express Handbook

- "Traits of Effective Writing," pages 18-23, is a useful reference for students as they develop their narratives.

- "Narrative Writing," pages 106-111, provides students with basic steps and models for this form of writing.

Writers Express Program Guide

- A teaching unit (lesson plans and blackline masters) can be found in the Program Guide ring binder for each grade level.

Friendly Notes and Letters

(See handbook pages 144-149.)

Everyone enjoys receiving personal mail. Think of how quickly you flip through the mail each day, passing over envelopes marked "Occupant," searching for a personal note. There is a joy in receiving friendly letters, a joy felt by children and adults alike. Letters have the power to make friendships stronger and draw family members closer together. And as this chapter states, "The best way to make sure you receive mail is to send some!"

Rationale

- Writing a friendly letter gives students the opportunity to express themselves freely.
- Receiving letters encourages students to write.
- Learning how to communicate in writing is an important social skill.

Major Concepts

- **A friendly letter has a heading, salutation, body, closing, and signature.** (pages 144-145)
- **E-mail is an electronic communication.** (page 147)
- **Invitations and thank-you notes have a salutation, body, closing, and signature.** (pages 148-149)

Performance Standards

Students are expected to . . .
- choose the appropriate form according to their purpose for writing, including journals, letters, poems, and narratives.
- correspond with peers or others via e-mail and conventional mail.

Getting Started with "Friendly Notes and Letters"

Start-Up Activity: This activity will engage students in "legal" note passing. Tell students they may take turns writing back and forth to a partner, using the same piece of paper. Their topic can be a current topic of study, a personal interest, or a classroom concern. During the activity, the students cannot talk, which turns their written messages into a "conversation." (Adapted from a strategy by Carolyn Burke.)

Enrichment Activity: As your students study people in science and social studies, use friendly letter writing as a report strategy. Let your students create a series of letters that these individuals might have received or sent at different points in their lives.

Teaching Resources

Writers Express Teacher's Guide

- Minilessons:

  Grade 4
  "Dear Occupant," (page 236)

  Grade 5
  "E-xciting" (page 236)

Writers Express Handbook

- "Writing-to-Learn Activities," page 355, suggests using "unsent letters" as a learning tool.

- "Writing a Letter to the Editor," pages 164-165, and "Business Writing," pages 176-181, give students practice in more formal kinds of letter writing.

Writers Express Program Guide

- A teaching unit (lesson plans and blackline masters) can be found in the Program Guide ring binder for each grade level.

Biographical Writing

(See handbook pages 151-155)

A biography usually tells the story of a person's entire life. Some types of biographical writing, however, present only part of a person's life. These pieces often take the form of a short story or a description of a person. They are called "biographical sketches" or "character sketches." When students write about others, they begin to discover an interesting world besides their own. In turn, they often learn to understand themselves better.

Rationale
- Biographical writing is a way of saving memories of another person.
- Writing about others helps children discover worlds beyond their own.
- Young people can learn to understand themselves by trying to understand others.

Major Concepts
- **Biographical writing is the sharing of correct and interesting information about a person.** (page 151)
- **The less a student knows about a subject, the more research will be required to compose a satisfactory biographical sketch.** (page 152)
- **Writing a biographical sketch calls for lots of interesting details about a subject**. (pages 153-155)

Performance Standards

Students are expected to . . .
- use anecdotes, descriptions, and vivid language to support the purpose of a written work.
- write narratives that contain a beginning, a middle, and an ending.
- write narratives that are enriched with details and personal feelings.

Getting Started with "Biographical Writing"

Start-Up Activity: There are many fine biographies written for children. Choose one and begin reading it to the class. As students work on their own biographical writing, do some comparing and contrasting of the elements in the published book and those in the students' work.

Enrichment Activity: Ask students to present their biographical sketches orally. They may read their stories, give short oral summaries, or even present little skits. Students who enjoy dramatic play may want to wear a hat or other clothing item suitable to their characters.

Teaching Resources

Writers Express Teacher's Guide

- Minilessons:

  Grade 4
  "What's so special?" (page 236)

  Grade 5
  "In the Spotlight" (page 236)
- "Assessment Strategies and Rubrics" (pages 183-184)

Writers Express Handbook

- "Traits of Effective Writing," pages 18-23, serves as a guide to students as they write their biographical stories.
- "Interviewing," page 159, gives students tips for gathering information directly from their subjects.

Writers Express Program Guide

- A teaching unit (lesson plans and blackline masters) can be found in the Program Guide ring binder for each grade level.

Writing Newspaper Stories

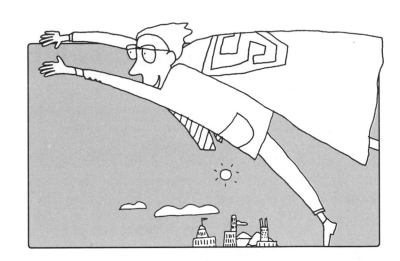

(See handbook pages 156-165.)

Journalists choose what to write about, gather information, decide which details to empha-size, and try to present readers with a clear and accurate finished story. The readers then interpret the story, knowing that journalists make choices and highlight what seems important to them. Accurate reporting is a responsibility.

Rationale
- Writing newspaper stories is important to young writers because there's an assumption that the writing will be published.
- Many of the qualities of good writing—focus, coherence, design, and clarity—are stressed in newswriting.

Major Concepts
- **Interviewing is fundamental to newswriting.** (page 159)
- **Basic news stories require a limited focus and coherent structure.** (page 162)
- **Feature stories, including human-interest stories, require good leads.** (pages 162-163)
- **Writing a letter to the editor is an important way to practice freedom of expression.** (pages 164-165)

Performance Standards

Students are expected to . . .
- include significant information in the body of the news story.
- select vocabulary and voice with an awareness of audience and purpose.
- use available technology to support aspects of creating, revising, editing, and publishing texts.

Getting Started with "Writing Newspaper Stories"

Start-Up Activity: Read about "Parts of a Newspaper Story," pages 160-161 in the handbook. Then have students look in a real newspaper for a news story. Challenge them to label the news story with the seven labels on page 160.

Enrichment Activity: Have students write a letter to the editor of the local newspaper, offering their opinions about something that they think needs changing. Direct them to use the format and directions for "Writing a Letter to the Editor" on pages 164-165.

Teaching Resources

Writers Express Teacher's Guide

*   Minilessons:

    Grade 4
    "For the Record" (page 236)

    Grade 5
    "Big News" (page 237)

Writers Express Handbook

*   "Descriptive Writing," pages 100-105, gives students ideas for collecting information about a person, a place, or an object.

*   "Writing Persuasive Essays," pages 94-99, offers students guidelines that transfer well to writing editorials.

*   "Research Your Subject," page 46, lists sources students can use to gather information for their newspaper stories.

Writers Express Program Guide

*   A teaching unit (lesson plans and blackline masters) can be found in the Program Guide ring binder for each grade level.

Writing Book Reviews

(See handbook pages 166-171.)

True readers relish book reviews because they love books and there's simply too much out there to read. Reviews help readers make decisions about the next books they will read. One reason people rush to get the Sunday edition of large-city newspapers is to read the book-review section. (Our goal is to create the same excitement for young readers and writers.)

Rationale

- Book reviews give students an opportunity to write about books they enjoy.
- Book reviews give students the opportunity to write persuasively.
- Developing book reviews brings the skills of reading and writing together to demonstrate students' comprehension of the text.

Major Concepts

- **A book review offers students an opportunity to respond to literature and to share literature with others.** (page 166)
- **A basic book review answers three questions: (1) What is the book about? (2) What do I like about this book? (3) What is the book's theme or message?** (pages 168-169)
- **Students can respond to literature in several ways.** (pages 170-171)

Performance Standards

Students are expected to . . .
- demonstrate an understanding of a literary work.
- include a summary that contains a main idea and significant details.
- support judgments through references to the text or to personal knowledge.
- punctuate titles correctly.

Getting Started with "Writing Book Reviews"

Start-Up Activity: Make a list of your five favorite books of all time. After each title, write down some things you liked about the book as well as what you learned from it. Post your list in the classroom, and encourage your students to create their own.

Enrichment Activity: As students read a novel, especially one with lots of historical details, have them keep notes in a journal. Encourage them to do this after each chapter, including the details they want to remember as well as comments, both positive and negative, about incidents in the story.

Teaching Resources

Writers Express Teacher's Guide

- Minilessons:

  Grade 4
  "A stitch in time . . ." (page 237)

  Grade 5
  "In a Nutshell" (page 237)

Writers Express Handbook

- "Using Writing Techniques," pages 124-127, presents and explains many concepts needed to understand and write about literature.

Writers Express Program Guide

- A teaching unit (lesson plans and blackline masters) can be found in the Program Guide ring binder for each grade level.

How-To Writing

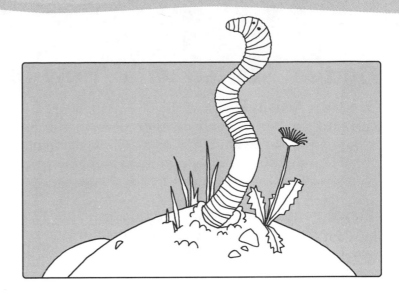

(See handbook pages 172-175.)

Students are often called upon to write explanations for many different reasons and in many different classes. In language arts, they may be asked to explain how to make something; in science, they may be asked to explain how a process works; in art, they may be asked to explain the steps they followed to complete a major project; and so on. Students may, in fact, be asked to write more explanations than any other form of writing throughout the curriculum.

Rationale

- Writing explanations helps students write clearly and sequentially.
- Writing explanations has practical applications—giving directions, describing scientific processes, explaining experiments, and so on.

Major Concepts

- **Explanations begin with a topic sentence (or a highly descriptive title), followed by clear, step-by-step directions.** (page 173)
- **The use of linking words (*first, next, then, finally,* etc.) makes explanations easy to follow.** (page 173)

Performance Standards

Students are expected to . . .
- include supporting paragraphs with simple facts, details, or step-by-step directions in their expository writing.
- use linking words for transitions.

Getting Started with "How-To Writing"

Start-Up Activity: Work with your class to write a detailed explanation of how to get from one place in your school to another place. (Set it up as a numbered list, much like "Save Our Wilderness" on the bottom of page 175 in the handbook.) Give these directions to a first- or second-grade class. Ask them to read and follow the directions. After they have followed the steps to the destination, greet them with a surprise treat.

Enrichment Activity: Choose a time period in history. Have students research and explain how people of that era completed a certain task, like crossing the plains, building a sod house, or panning for gold. Another option is to have them explain how people in another country do an activity differently than they do (games and sports are good subjects).

Teaching Resources

Writers Express Teacher's Guide

- Minilessons:

  Grade 4
  "Quadrilateral" (page 237)

  Grade 5
  "That's disgusting!" (page 237)

Writers Express Handbook

- "Sample Expository Paragraph," page 80, explains the basics of expository writing and provides tips on organization.

- "Putting Things in Order," page 84, helps students to recognize and choose the best form of organization for their how-to writing.

- "Transition Words," page 85, lists terms that students can use to make their writing flow smoothly from step to step.

Writers Express Program Guide

- A teaching unit (lesson plans and blackline masters) can be found in the Program Guide ring binder for each grade level.

Business Writing

(See handbook pages 176-183.)

When students write business letters, they have the opportunity to communicate in a business-like way. They usually enjoy this form of writing for two reasons: It makes them feel grown-up, and they enjoy receiving serious responses. In a similar but less formal way, writing memos gives students real business-writing experience.

Rationale

- The business letter is a form of writing that students can use to get information or request action.
- When students receive serious responses to their letters, they learn that they can cause changes.
- The ability to write a clear business letter or memo will serve students now and throughout their lives.

Major Concepts

- **A business letter is more formal, or serious, than a friendly letter.** (pages 176-177)
- **The business letter format includes the heading, inside address, salutation, body, closing, and signature.** (pages 178-180)
- **There is an accepted way to fold and address business letters.** (page 181)
- **A memo is a common form of business writing.** (pages 182-183)

Performance Standards

Students are expected to . . .
- choose the appropriate form according to their purpose for writing a letter.
- consider the audience, purpose, and context of a letter.
- include all parts of a letter.
- use a correctly addressed envelope.

Getting Started with "Business Writing"

Start-Up Activity: Discuss three or four specific topics that you will be covering in your science and social studies classes. Then brainstorm for names of people in the community who could share information or do a demonstration related to these topics. Assign students to write to these people, asking them to send information and/or visit the classroom.

Enrichment Activity: Once students are comfortable with the form of a business letter, ask them to be responsible for classroom correspondence. Invite students who are interested to take turns responding to classroom visitors, sending letters of thanks or complaint, or writing to the editors of book clubs, magazines, and newspapers.

Teaching Resources

Writers Express Teacher's Guide

- Minilessons:
  Grade 4
  " 'For Matt' " (page 238)
  Grade 5
  "Don't forget." (page 238)

Writers Express Handbook

- "Sample E-Mail Message," page 147, shows students a model of a type of writing used frequently in today's business world.
- "Writing On-Line," page 266, and "Netiquette," page 267, give students tips and guidelines for writing, sending, and receiving e-mail.

Writers Express Program Guide

- A teaching unit (lesson plans and blackline masters) can be found in the Program Guide ring binder for each grade level.

Writing a Summary

(See handbook pages 185-187.)

When students write summaries, they learn to identify the main ideas in reading material and how to present those ideas clearly and simply. Summarizing is a very effective writing-to-learn technique, one that helps students personalize or internalize learning, so they understand better and remember longer.

Rationale

- Summarizing helps students process information.
- The ability to write summaries can be applied to longer pieces such as book reviews, classroom reports, and news stories.
- Writing summaries promotes higher-level thinking skills.

Major Concepts

- **Summarizing is easier for students if they read and write with a plan in mind.** (pages 185-186)
- **Summaries need to be written in the student's own words.** (pages 186-187)
- **The structure of a summary is similar to the paragraph, including a topic sentence and supporting details.** (pages 186-187)

Performance Standards

Students are expected to . . .
- develop a topic sentence.
- include supporting information.
- arrange ideas in a logical order.

Getting Started with "Writing a Summary"

Start-Up Activity: To introduce students to the concept of summarizing, try a "sentence summary." Write the following long sentence (66 words) on the chalkboard, project it on an overhead, or duplicate it on half sheets for each student.

> After the long day's drive to Yellowstone Park, the girls helped their dad unpack the tent and campstove, the rolls of sleeping bags, the duffel bags of clothes, the boxes of food, and the containers of water, but as they hoisted the canoe off the roof of the car, Mom suddenly called out that something was missing—the canvas bag containing the tent poles and stakes.

Then ask students to identify the main idea. Have them condense the sentence to half the number of words (33) and keep its meaning. Then ask them to pare it down again to about half that number of words. Finally, ask them how few words they can use and still keep the main idea of this sentence.

Enrichment Activity: Your students can practice their summarizing skills by writing one-paragraph summaries of recent class events to be published in a class newsletter. Consider subjects as varied as birthday celebrations, science experiments, history lessons, and class visitors.

Teaching Resources

Writers Express Teacher's Guide

- Minilessons:
  Grades 4 and 5
  "In summary . . . " (page 238)

Writers Express Handbook

- "Improving Viewing Skills," pages 324-329, includes a sample summary of a television special.

Writers Express Program Guide

- A teaching unit (lesson plans and blackline masters) can be found in the Program Guide ring binder for each grade level.

Writing Observation Reports

(See handbook pages 188-191.)

Young people are natural observers. They notice everything, ask lots of questions, and enjoy discovering the world around them. This chapter taps into students' natural curiosity and requires them to use all of their senses to observe and then write—in language arts and across the curriculum.

Rationale	• Attention to detail is an important writing skill.
	• Observing and recording details offers students a treasury of writing ideas.
	• Improving observation skills is especially important in science classes.

Major Concepts	• **Descriptive writing requires the use of all the senses.** (pages 188-189)
	• **Sensory details in writing enrich the reader's experience.** (pages 190-191)

Performance Standards

Students are expected to . . .
• establish a central idea for a report.
• include a variety of sensory details.

Getting Started with "Writing Observation Reports"

Start-Up Activity: Begin by reading "A Visit to Fort Laramie," handbook page 190. Then, using a period of history you are currently studying, ask students to pretend they are present at an event from that period. As they imagine "being there," have them list the sights, sounds, and smells of the event. Conduct a sharing session.

Enrichment Activity: Using the sample "Science Observation Report" on page 191 in the handbook, assign a similar activity using a current science topic. Remind students to use their senses to gather details for their reports.

Teaching Resources

Writers Express Teacher's Guide

- Minilessons:
  Grade 4
  "Recess rocks!" (page 238)
  Grade 5
  "Sharpened Senses" (page 238)

Writers Express Handbook

- "Descriptive Writing," pages 100-105, gives students tips on observing and gathering details for their reports.

- "Writing a Classroom Report," pages 192-203, is a logical "next step" after students write observation reports.

Writers Express Program Guide

- A teaching unit (lesson plans and blackline masters) can be found in the Program Guide ring binder for each grade level.

Writing a Classroom Report

(See handbook pages 192-203.)

A report is a collection of facts and other information (such as true stories and quotations) about a selected topic. Reports can take many forms—student-made booklets on various topics for a classroom library, chapters about different wild animals for a classroom anthology about the natural world, oral reports, and so on. A well-written report should be interesting, clear, and accurate.

Rationale
- Writing reports will teach students about organizing nonfiction.
- Many students will have to write nonfiction as adults. Developing report-writing skills now will prepare them for this task.
- Students are naturally curious. When they are allowed to choose their own topics, they find report writing interesting and enjoyable.

Major Concepts
- **Selecting a topic requires much thought.** (pages 192-193)
- **A report should answer questions the writer wants answered.** (pages 194-195)
- **Using gathering grids, note cards, and outlines helps students organize information for their reports.** (pages 195-197)
- **A report should have a strong beginning, an informative middle, and a well-crafted ending.** (pages 198-200)
- **A formal report requires proper documentation.** (pages 201-203)

Performance Standards

Students are expected to . . .
- establish a central idea/topic for a report.
- support the central idea with facts, details, examples, and explanations.
- include a beginning, a middle, and an ending in their reports.

Getting Started with "Writing a Classroom Report"

Start-Up Activity: Since writing a report involves gathering lots of information, work with the students to list places and ways to get information. After the list is as long as you can make it, take students to the library to see if there are any other possibilities. Encourage students to use as many sources as possible for their class reports.

Enrichment Activity: Encourage your students to search out quotations, stories, colorful words, interesting diagrams and drawings, and humorous or surprising information to enhance their report writing. Then be sure to share different ways this information can be used in their reports.

Teaching Resources

Writers Express Teacher's Guide

- Minilessons:
  Grade 4
  "Nitty 'Griddy' " (page 239)
  Grade 5
  "Going Batty" (page 239)

Writers Express Handbook

- "Writing with Computers," pages 24-29, gives tips about writing and designing written work.
- "Using the Library," pages 255-263, has many practical guidelines for students who will be doing research in the library.

Writers Express Program Guide

- A teaching unit (lesson plans and blackline masters) can be found in the Program Guide ring binder for each grade level.

Multimedia Computer Reports

(See handbook pages 204-207.)

From interactive articles on CD, to hypertext pages on the World Wide Web, to computer "slide shows" in business meetings, multimedia presentations are permeating our culture. Learning to create a multimedia report is of great value to today's students. Fortunately, the skills required are not difficult to learn.

Rationale

- Tomorrow's scholars and business people must be able to use computers to write their reports and deliver their presentations.
- Multimedia reports provide an opportunity for writing practice.
- Preparing a multimedia report is generally a high-interest project for students.

Major Concepts

- **There are two types of multimedia computer reports: the multimedia presentation and the interactive report.** (page 204)
- **An interactive report is a hypertext document like an encyclopedia entry on CD.** (page 205)
- **A multimedia presentation is like a computer "slide show" used to support a speech.** (page 206)
- **A storyboard helps to plan either type of multimedia computer report.** (page 207)

Performance Standards

Students are expected to . . .
- choose the appropriate form according to their purpose for writing or presenting.
- use available technology to support aspects of creating, revising, editing, and publishing texts.

Getting Started with "Multimedia Computer Reports"

Start-Up Activity: Using an overview of the chapter, discuss with students the reasons behind creating a multimedia report. Address the importance of multimedia presentations in businesses (advertisers, companies with a new product, etc.). Then talk about how this kind of presentation can be used in school.

Enrichment Activity: Remind students that a multimedia report can be as complicated as using two computers and a prerecorded sound track, or as simple as a demonstration of a dance step using taped music. Have small groups of students plan a multimedia computer presentations for a report or a speech that you provide. Then have the groups discuss their storyboards and see how differently the groups planned to present the same material.

Teaching Resources

Writers Express Teacher's Guide
- "Writing for Specific Subject Areas" (pages 175-176)

Writers Express Handbook
- "Giving Speeches," pages 311-317, provides the speech used as the basis for the multimedia report in this chapter.

Writers Express Program Guide
- A teaching unit (lesson plans and blackline masters) can be found in the Program Guide ring binder for each grade level.

Writing Fantasies

(See handbook pages 209-215.)

Games of make-believe and pretend are popular with children of all ages. Nancy Bond, an author of many popular fantasies, says phrases such as *Let's pretend, I wish I were . . . , I wish I had . . . ,* and *What would happen if . . . ?* serve as starting points for millions of stories.

Rationale
- When writing fantasy stories, young writers use their imaginations to develop characters, problems, and solutions.
- Through fantasy, students can explore some of the great themes in literature, including the struggle between good and evil, the ability to overcome obstacles with faith and perseverance, and the power of love and friendship.

Major Concepts
- **In fantasy stories anything can happen, as long as it's believable within the story's overall context.** (page 212)
- **A fantasy needs characters, a problem to solve, and a setting.** (page 213)
- **Revising involves time away from a story, a chance to make certain it's believable in context, and the opportunity to share a draft and get feedback.** (page 214)

Performance Standards

Students are expected to . . .
- establish characters, a problem, and a setting.
- use dialogue in support of stories.
- share finished work with classmates and others.

Getting Started with "Writing Fantasies"

Start-Up Activity: On their own, have students list some of their favorite books and stories from childhood. (Many of these will probably be animal fantasies.) Then come together and talk about the elements of fantasy—a story in which something impossible is accepted as real. Finally, have students decide which of their favorite books and stories are fantasies.

Enrichment Activity: Introduce the idea of writing autobiographical fantasies. Ask students to imagine what their lives as adults will be like, or ask them to pretend to be 75 years old, looking back on their lives. Whether these autobiographies are realistic or outrageous—they'll have an element of fantasy.

Teaching Resources

Writers Express Teacher's Guide

- Minilessons:

  Grade 4
  "Shooting Star" (page 239)

  Grade 5
  "Just pretend." (page 239)

- "Assessment Strategies and Rubrics" (pages 183-184)

Writers Express Handbook

- "Writing with Style," pages 122-131, introduces writing techniques students will use to enliven their fantasies.

- "Publishing Your Writing," pages 68-73, provides guidelines and tips for students wanting to share their fantasies outside the classroom.

Writers Express Program Guide

- A teaching unit (lesson plans and blackline masters) can be found in the Program Guide ring binder for each grade level.

Writing Tall Tales

(See handbook pages 216-219.)

None of us would be hard-pressed to name a time when we exaggerated to make a point. Remember the "big fish" story? It's the one that goes, "I caught a fish the likes of which you won't believe!" It's always told with arms stretched out at least two feet. Fortunately, the human tendency to exaggerate serves the tall-tale writer well.

Rationale
- Tall-tale writing gives students' imaginations free rein.
- The necessity for exaggeration and humor entices even reluctant writers.
- In tall tales, students are able to play with language and situations, stretching them beyond their usual boundaries.

Major Concepts
- **Tall tales incorporate exaggeration and humor.** (pages 216-217)
- **Tall tales require especially descriptive language.** (pages 218-219)

Performance Standards

Students are expected to . . .
- establish characters, a problem, and a setting.
- enrich their writing with details, dialogue, and figures of speech.
- edit drafts to ensure standard usage, varied sentence structure, appropriate word choice, correct spelling, capitalization, punctuation, and format.

Getting Started with "Writing Tall Tales"

Start-Up Activity: Begin by reviewing some of the writing techniques—especially exaggeration and personification—listed in "Using Writing Techniques," handbook pages 124-127. Next, read aloud "Musky Mike's Big Catch," handbook page 217. Then read the story a second time, asking students to raise their hands each time they hear exaggeration or personification used. If time permits, repeat this activity with other tall tales.

Enrichment Activity: Have each student select a historical figure to serve as the main character of a short (one-paragraph) tall tale. Students' paragraphs should focus on one experience or adventure that this character would probably have had. Share finished stories with the class.

Teaching Resources

Writers Express Teacher's Guide

- Minilessons:
  Grade 4
  "He lassoed Texas!" (page 239)
  Grade 5
  "You're incredible!" (page 240)
- "Assessment Strategies and Rubrics" (pages 183-184)

Writers Express Handbook

- In "Using Writing Techniques," pages 124-127, students will find definitions and examples of exaggeration and personification.

- "A Strategy for Reading Fiction," page 276, provides a sample plot line to guide students as they write their tall tales.

Writers Express Program Guide

- A teaching unit (lesson plans and blackline masters) can be found in the Program Guide ring binder for each grade level.

Writing Realistic Stories

(See handbook pages 220-225.)

Anything is possible in realistic fiction as long as it seems true, could be true, but hasn't actually happened. Author Sandy Asher says, "In realistic fiction, characters find their own realistic solutions. And their search teaches them—and their readers—something worth knowing about real life."

Rationale
- Writing realistic stories helps students better understand the fiction-writing process.
- Writing realistic stories helps students appreciate that ideas for writing can come from their own lives.

Major Concepts
- **The characters and problems in realistic fiction may be based on real life.** (pages 220-221)
- **It helps to think about the main elements in a story before writing it.** (page 222)
- **Students can begin a realistic story with a question, dialogue, description, or background information.** (page 223)
- **Realistic characters solve their problems in believable ways.** (page 223)

Performance Standards

Students are expected to . . .
- establish believable characters, problems, and settings.
- use dialogue in stories.
- edit drafts to ensure standard usage, varied sentence structure, appropriate word choice, correct spelling, capitalization, punctuation, and format.

Getting Started with "Writing Realistic Stories"

Start-Up Activity: With the class, read or tell a story about a real inventor, doctor, or scientist. Discuss the problems the person faced and the solutions he or she devised. Decide if there are some fictional elements that would make the story more exciting.

Enrichment Activity: Take a passage from a realistic story that contains dialogue, and rewrite it without the dialogue. Read both versions to the class; then engage students in a discussion about the overall impact of both versions. What are the effects of interesting, realistic dialogue in a story?

Teaching Resources

Writers Express Teacher's Guide

- Minilessons:

  Grade 4
  "Deposit another quarter." (page 240)

  Grade 5
  "Get Real" (page 240)

- "Assessment Strategies and Rubrics" (pages 183-184)

Writers Express Handbook

- "Gathering Story Ideas," page 140, guides students in their search for characters and situations to write about.

- "Narrative Writing," pages 106-111, gives students basic guidelines for story writing.

Writers Express Program Guide

- A teaching unit (lesson plans and blackline masters) can be found in the Program Guide ring binder for each grade level.

Writing Stories from History

(See handbook pages 226-231.)

Historical tales must be believable to be interesting, and so they must be founded on the truth about a particular time, or at least on what could have happened in a certain period. This kind of writing has the potential for making history truly interesting to students.

Rationale
- Writing stories from history requires students to delve into the past, exploring a person, an era, or an event.
- The study of history becomes more real and more interesting to students as they read, and write, about a given period from history.

Major Concepts
- **Historical stories may be about real people or about fictional characters who could have lived during a certain time.** (page 227)
- **Students can collect accurate information about a historical period (and its people) by reading and by talking with teachers and librarians.** (page 228)
- **It's important to identify the main elements in a story before writing the first draft.** (page 229)

Performance Standards

Students are expected to . . .
- establish historical characters, a problem, and a setting.
- establish a topic, key ideas, or events in sequence and/or chronological order.
- edit drafts to ensure standard usage, varied sentence structure, appropriate word choice, correct spelling, capitalization, punctuation, and format.

Getting Started with "Writing Stories from History"

Start-Up Activity: Ask students to recall subjects (people and events) from history that interest them. Make a list of their suggestions. Have each student choose a person or an event and write freely about that subject for 3-5 minutes. Then explore ways that students can both check and acquire more information about their subjects.

Enrichment Activity: On the board, draw a time line from the approximate year of birth of your students to the present. Ask students to suggest historical happenings (either general or personal) to include on the time line. Invite them to write short stories, placing themselves in one of these historical events.

Teaching Resources

Writers Express Teacher's Guide

- Minilessons:

  Grade 4
  "Westward Ho!" (page 240)

  Grade 5
  "Way-Back Machine" (page 240)

- "Assessment Strategies and Rubrics" (pages 183-184)

Writers Express Handbook

- "Writing a Classroom Report," pages 192-197, offers students tips on searching for, gathering, and organizing information.

- "Descriptive Writing," pages 100-105, helps students to adequately present the settings for their stories from history.

- "Using the Library," pages 255-263, and "Researching on the Internet," page 268, guide students in their search for historical facts for their stories.

Writers Express Program Guide

- A teaching unit (lesson plans and blackline masters) can be found in the Program Guide ring binder for each grade level.

Writing Plays

(See handbook pages 232-237.)

No matter who writes it—a student or a professional writer—the basic elements of a play remain the same: The main character solves a problem or reaches an important goal through action. The excitement and fun of playwriting is enhanced by the possibility that the work will be read aloud or performed.

Rationale

- When writing plays, children can draw on their natural ability to role-play. This gives them practice in using the language, thinking logically, and being part of a group.
- Learning more about playwriting can lead to an appreciation of drama, an important form of literature.

Major Concepts

- **Plays begin with characters who need to solve a problem or reach a goal.** (pages 232-233)
- **Playwrights follow a specific format.** (pages 233-237)
- **Writers often discover what their characters will do and say, as they write.** (pages 234-235)
- **Good dialogue is the most important part of playwriting.** (page 236)
- **Plays usually make a point. As young writers write and revise, this point (the theme) helps them decide what to keep and what to put aside.** (pages 236-237)

Performance Standards - - - - - -

Students are expected to . . .
- establish characters, a problem, and a setting for a play.
- use action to solve a problem.
- create dialogue for characters.

Getting Started with "Writing Plays"

Start-Up Activity: Reader's theater is an informal kind of playwriting. Students can quite easily turn a favorite chapter from a novel into a reader's theater production. Ask small groups of students who have read the same novel to choose a chapter—one with lots of dialogue—and prepare a script. (They could use a format similar to the one shown on handbook page 233. Remind students that they may include "stage directions" in parentheses, too.)

Enrichment Activity: Classroom reports about topics that involve solving problems or reaching goals have playwriting potential. Topics such as farming the ocean, caring for our neighborhoods, and respecting people's differences have great script potential. Groups working on related topics could write a play together.

Teaching Resources

Writers Express Teacher's Guide

- Minilessons:

  Grade 4
  " 'Exit, stage right!' " (page 241)

  Grade 5
  " 'The raccoon did it!' " (page 241)

Writers Express Handbook

- "Why Write?" (page 1) gives an example of how some students gathered information, wrote a play, and enjoyed their success.

- "Sample Plot Line," page 276, guides students as they develop their own story lines.

Writers Express Program Guide

- A teaching unit (lesson plans and blackline masters) can be found in the Program Guide ring binder for each grade level.

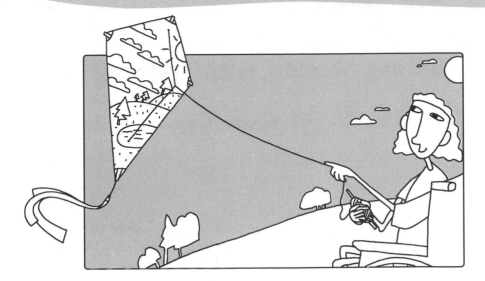

Writing Poems

(See handbook pages 239-249)

Writing poetry is a child's invitation to play with language. Poetry has many forms—some are very free and some are formulaic. As children listen to and respond to poetry, they will learn about the different shapes it can take. Poet Anne-Marie Oomen says, "I write poems when I feel what I have to say needs a special shape and sound."

Rationale

- Writing poetry gives students an opportunity to better understand this form of writing.
- Writing poetry offers students an especially creative avenue for exploring and expressing their ideas.
- Students learn to choose words purposefully and use figures of speech.
- Students learn that the sounds of words can help to convey meaning.

Major Concepts

- **Poetry is filled with word pictures and pleasing sounds.** (pages 239-241)
- **Poets often speak from personal experience and write in free verse.** (pages 242-245)
- **Poetry uses special writing devices, including figures of speech.** (page 245)
- **There are many types of traditional poems.** (pages 246-247)
- **Playful poetry includes a variety of new, creative forms.** (pages 248-249)

Performance Standards

Students are expected to . . .
- include figures of speech in their poems.
- pay attention to sound and arrangement of words in poems.
- become aware of the power of language in poetry.

Getting Started with "Writing Poems"

Start-Up Activity: Read aloud some of the poems from this chapter or from a favorite book of poetry. Write one of these poems on a chart or on the chalkboard. Ask students to point out the elements that make poetry a special form of writing. Write a class poem about a topic relevant for the students. (Consider using a free-verse or playful form, rather than traditional.)

Enrichment Activity: "Five W's Poetry," handbook page 248, and "Cinquain," handbook page 246, are two forms of poetry that lend themselves to writing about people or places. Ask students to use these forms to write about people or places they know well. Remind them that this task will require the same information they would put in a simple paragraph.

Teaching Resources

Writers Express Teacher's Guide

- Minilessons:
  Grade 4
  "Color me glad." (page 241)
  Grade 5
  "Prose into Poetry" (page 241)

Writers Express Handbook

- "Publishing Your Writing," pages 68-73, gives students ideas and outlets for sharing their poetry.

- "Using Writing Techniques," pages 124-127, defines and illustrates many of the writing techniques poets use.

- "Performing Poems," pages 318-323, is a natural follow-up to "Writing Poems."

Writers Express Program Guide

- A teaching unit (lesson plans and blackline masters) can be found in the Program Guide ring binder for each grade level.

Writing Riddles

(See handbook pages 250-253.)

What makes riddles fun to write and funny to hear? Riddle writers say it's wordplay—words playing with one another and with you. This chapter offers several techniques students can use to write riddles. It also encourages them to use their imaginations. Students can go wild searching for puns and outlandish metaphors.

Rationale
- Students will discover the fun of writing riddles.
- Writing riddles gives students a creative outlet for using puns and figures of speech.
- Writing riddles increases vocabulary.

Major Concepts
- **Writing riddles is a form of mental exercise.** (page 250)
- **Riddles can incorporate homophones, homographs, and two figures of speech—personification and metaphor.** (pages 251-252)
- **Students use metaphors, personification, and comparison to write riddles.** (pages 251-253)

Performance Standards - - - - - -

Students are expected to . . .
- become aware of the power of language.
- use figures of speech in their writing.

Getting Started with "Writing Riddles"

Start-Up Activity: Give students a list of two-word riddles. You will give them one-word synonyms for each word in the answer. The answer to the riddle must be two rhyming words. For example: "distant auto" is a "far car." After several examples, students should be able to create their own riddles. Here are several examples: "cottage rodent" is a "house mouse," "unripe vegetable" is a "green bean," "encyclopedia corner" is a "book nook." The class can play as a whole or gather in small groups. Share the best riddles with the entire class. Encourage students to take this activity home to share with family and friends.

Enrichment Activity: Some students might enjoy writing riddles with almost-sound-alike words. Here are some examples: verse/worse; tuba/tube of; bacon/bakin'; oily/early; porpoise/purpose; fur/for. Here's an example from *Funny You Should Ask* by Marvin Terban:

What do you call a pirate ship?

"A thug boat" (*Sounds like tugboat.*)

Teaching Resources

Writers Express Teacher's Guide

- Minilessons:

  Grades 4 and 5
  "Why is a ___ like a ___?" (page 241)

Writers Express Handbook

- "Building Vocabulary Skills," pages 288-305, helps students develop the language skills necessary for writing and solving riddles.

- "Analyzing," page 342, and "Synthesizing," page 343, guide students in the thinking processes used to create and enjoy writing riddles.

Writers Express Program Guide

- A teaching unit (lesson plans and blackline masters) can be found in the Program Guide ring binder for each grade level.

The Tools of Learning

Introductory Notes

This section introduces "The Tools of Learning" chapters in the handbook and provides getting-started ideas to help you with your initial planning.

Using the Library

(See handbook pages 255-263.)

Students may know where in the library to find their favorite mysteries or sports stories, but information on the constellations or volcanoes often eludes them. As teachers, we must encourage a friendly "relationship" between the library and our students.

Rationale
- Libraries, whether traditional or on-line, continue to be storehouses of knowledge that students must know how to access.
- Knowing how to find and use the library's resources is an invaluable skill for all students.
- Familiarity with the library will help ensure its productive use.

Major Concepts
- **The library is a place where students "meet" experts and "hear" stories through books, magazines, CD-ROM's, videos, and so on.** (page 255)
- **Knowing how to use a computer catalog and/or a card catalog will help students find specific books.** (pages 256-258)
- **Understanding the arrangement of books on shelves will help students find specific books and periodicals.** (page 259)
- **The encyclopedia (book form or CD) serves as a starting place for finding general information on any topic.** (page 260)
- **Reference books contain interesting, up-to-date information.** (page 261)
- **Knowing the parts of nonfiction books helps students use them efficiently.** (page 262)
- **The *Children's Magazine Guide* offers special information of interest to students.** (page 263)

Performance Standards

Students are expected to . . .
- use print and electronic sources to locate books and articles.
- locate information in the library.
- use various reference materials as an aid to writing.

Getting Started with "Using the Library"

Start-Up Activity: Assign students to be library guides who, using the information in this chapter, along with their own familiarity with the school library, help younger students find their way around the library. Be sure to collaborate with the librarian for this activity.

Enrichment Activity: Remind students that the research they do for their writing should be up-to-date. Help them understand that recent magazine articles or sites on the Internet will often give them the most current information. Devise a short lesson on using the *Children's Magazine Guide*.

Teaching Resources

Writers Express Teacher's Guide

- Minilessons:

  Grade 4
  "Bookworm" (page 242)

  Grade 5
  "Snooping Around" (page 242)

Writers Express Handbook

- "Using the Internet," pages 264-269, introduces and explains this important source of information.

Writers Express Program Guide

- A teaching unit (lesson plans and blackline masters) can be found in the Program Guide ring binder for each grade level.

Using the Internet

(See handbook pages 264-269.)

The Internet allows writers to research current information more easily than ever before. It also connects them to a worldwide community of writers and gives them new opportunities to publish their writing. However, students must acquire certain skills to do that research, make those connections, and publish their writing.

Rationale

- Internet skills are essential for today's citizens.
- The immediacy of e-mail exchanges enhances the sense of writing as discourse.
- Real-world activities, such as submitting writing for Web publication or building a Web site, get students interested and involved.

Major Concepts

- **The Internet is more than just the World Wide Web.** (pages 264-265)
- **Writing on-line requires attention to detail and "Netiquette."** (pages 266-267)
- **Internet research involves applying navigation skills, using search engines, and knowing how to save information.** (page 268)
- **The Net offers students several options for publishing.** (page 269)

Performance Standards

Students are expected to . . .
- use available technology to support aspects of creating, revising, editing, and publishing texts.

Getting Started with "Using the Internet"

Start-Up Activity: Demonstrate the use of a family-friendly search engine (examples are <yahooligans.com> and <www.edview.com>). Show students how to narrow the scope of their inquiry to get more exact responses. Most search engines have an on-line tutorial, which may be helpful to go through with the whole class.

Enrichment Activity: Try this activity to demonstrate how a search engine works: You are an Internet user, and you want information on the Cyclops Polyphemus, but you're not sure how to spell Polyphemus. The students are the search engines; have them use a dictionary to find words that start with *"poly."* To narrow the search, ask them to find only those words that start with *"poly"* plus an *f* ("polyf"). To narrow it again, have them find only words that begin with *"polyph."* As you're doing this, explain that a search engine works the same way— it looks for everything that is even remotely related to your original search request. Therefore, the more specific you can be, the better your search-engine results will be.

Teaching Resources

Writers Express Teacher's Guide

- Minilessons:

  Grades 4 and 5
  "Logging On" (page 242)

Writers Express Handbook

- "Writing with Computers," pages 24-29, gives students tips for using computers and saving their files.

- "Sample E-Mail Message," page 147, and "Writing a Memo," pages 182-183, demonstrate how students and businesspeople correspond on-line.

Writers Express Program Guide

- A teaching unit (lesson plans and blackline masters) can be found in the Program Guide ring binder for each grade level.

Using Reading Strategies

(See handbook pages 271-279.)

To improve reading comprehension, students must become active readers, able to accommodate new information and determine which concepts are important. Reading is a strategic process, and active readers know how to draw from prior knowledge, interact with written text, react to new information, and create their own understanding of the material.

Rationale
- Students can learn new strategies for becoming active, thoughtful readers.
- Many students are capable yet inefficient readers. They may spend excessive time decoding proper nouns, fail to use context to discover meaning, or neglect to vary their reading speed.
- Strategic reading is used when retention is important—especially for studying.

Major Concepts
- **Good readers understand and remember important information.** (page 271)
- **There are many strategies for comprehending a text, and good readers use them before, during, and after reading.** (pages 272-276)
- **Reading strategies can be modeled/taught/learned in the context of classroom reading instruction.** (pages 272-276)
- **Knowing the elements of fiction and the types of literature gives students the vocabulary they need to talk about their reading.** (pages 277-279)

Performance Standards
Students are expected to . . .
- exhibit careful reading and understanding of a text.

Getting Started with "Using Reading Strategies"

Start-Up Activity: Introduce students to "Think and Read Strategy," handbook page 272. Then, in pairs, have them apply this strategy to a chapter or shorter section in one of their textbooks. During this activity, they should have their handbooks open and refer to them as needed.

Enrichment Activity: After students have learned about reading strategies, have them apply different strategies when they are reading. As an alternative response activity, after reading, have them try "Notes to the Teacher" or "Unsent Letters," handbook page 355.

Teaching Resources

Writers Express Teacher's Guide

- Minilessons:

  Grade 4
  "Feelings" (page 242)

  Grade 5
  "KWL" (page 243)

Writers Express Handbook

- "Writing as a Learning Tool," pages 353-355, offers writing suggestions that strengthen reading skills.

- "Building Vocabulary Skills," pages 288-305, includes a number of strategies related to acquiring a broader vocabulary.

Writers Express Program Guide

- A teaching unit (lesson plans and blackline masters) can be found in the Program Guide ring binder for each grade level.

Reading Graphics

(See handbook pages 280-287.)

"Reading graphics" means understanding symbols, signs, diagrams, and other kinds of pictures that convey information. Information pictures, such as hieroglyphics, are among the oldest forms of written communication. Graphs, which represent information only, were invented about 200 years ago.

Rationale
- Students must learn to interpret commonly used forms of written communication. Newspapers, magazines, advertisements, and TV news programs, as well as textbooks, use graphs, tables, symbols, and other graphics.
- The skills needed to "read" visually presented information differ from those needed to read printed information.

Major Concepts
- **Pictures, like words, are a form of communication.** (pages 280-287)
- **A picture, in most cases, means the same thing to everyone, while written and spoken language varies from region to region.** (pages 280- 281)
- **The most basic type of graphic is a symbol, or sign.** (page 281)
- **A diagram is like a map of an object or a set of objects.** (page 282)
- **A graph is a picture of information rather than a picture of objects.** (pages 283-285)
- **A table uses rows and columns to show how different kinds of information relate to each other.** (pages 286-287)

Performance Standards
Students are expected to . . .
- present information in various forms.

Getting Started with "Reading Graphics"

Start-Up Activity: Have students find different kinds of symbols in their science and math textbooks. Ask them to create a symbol page for each subject—showing symbols and their meanings. Another option is to conduct a class project, assigning groups of students to create a bulletin board of subject-related symbols and their meanings.

Enrichment Activity: Have students draw a picture diagram of something they are studying in one of their subjects: for example, a plant, an animal, or a simple machine or device. Have them use the object itself (or a photograph) as their model. Remind students to show and label the important parts.

Teaching Resources

Writers Express Teacher's Guide

- Minilessons:

  Grade 4
  "A picture is worth . . ." (page 243)

  Grade 5
  "Everybody line up." (page 243)

Writers Express Handbook

- "Student Almanac," pages 436-487, includes various charts and graphics for students to practice reading.

Writers Express Program Guide

- A teaching unit (lesson plans and blackline masters) can be found in the Program Guide ring binder for each grade level.

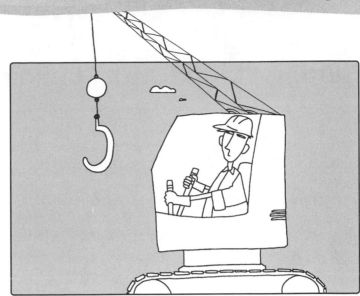

Building Vocabulary Skills

(See handbook pages 288-305.)

Learning the meanings of new words is very important for students. The stronger their vocabularies, the more they will learn from what they read and hear. In addition, students with solid vocabularies are better independent learners.

Rationale

- Vocabulary knowledge is fundamental to reading comprehension; students cannot understand a text without knowing most of its words.
- Strategies for increasing vocabulary can help students become more independent learners.

Major Concepts

- **Students' reading, writing, and speaking skills improve as their vocabularies increase.** (page 288)
- **There are several ways to read and check for the meanings of new words.** (page 289)
- **A dictionary and a thesaurus are important vocabulary-building resources.** (pages 290-292)
- **Students can make personal dictionaries to help them learn new words.** (page 293)
- **Understanding word parts and word families can help students figure out the meanings of unfamiliar words.** (pages 294-304)
- **There are formal and informal ways to use words.** (page 305)

Performance Standards

Students are expected to . . .
- use resources to find correct spellings, synonyms, and replacement words.

Getting Started with "Building Vocabulary Skills"

Start-Up Activity: Have students write words that contain these roots: *bio, geo, mem, photo,* and *therm.* (The root can fall anywhere in the word.) Using the words they have listed, ask students to guess the meaning of each root. After some discussion, have them check pages 298-304 in their handbooks for verification.

Enrichment Activity: Vocabulary games and activities like crossword puzzles and word finds are available in newspapers, on the Internet, and in many books. Use these as models for students to create their own vocabulary activities. When appropriate, have students share their activities with the class.

Teaching Resources

Writers Express Teacher's Guide

- Minilessons:

  Grade 4
  "They're related." (page 243)

  Grade 5
  "A What-ologist?" (page 244)

Writers Express Handbook

- "Checking for Word Choice," page 66, provides students with tips about choosing the best words for their writing.

- "Use Vocabulary Words Correctly," page 305, discusses formal and informal language.

Writers Express Program Guide

- A teaching unit (lesson plans and blackline masters) can be found in the Program Guide ring binder for each grade level.

Becoming a Better Speller

(See handbook pages 306-309.)

Teachers should have high expectations for proper spelling. Students must learn to spell an ever-growing number of words correctly and automatically as they write. In rough drafts and journal entries, students can take risks with spelling; but they must also learn how to find correct spellings for more formal pieces of writing. Students need to care about spelling for the right reason: readability of their work.

Rationale	• Learning to spell is closely tied to learning to read and write.
	• Proper spelling is an essential part of any formal writing.
Major Concepts	• **Students can use strategies to become better spellers.** (pages 306-309)
	• **Students can use the senses of sight, hearing, and touch to improve their spelling.** (page 307)
	• **Proofreading for spelling is part of the writing process.** (page 308)
	• **Knowing a few basic spelling rules can help students avoid common errors.** (page 309)

Performance Standards - - - - -

Students are expected to . . .
- spell accurately in final drafts.
- spell prefixes, suffixes, contractions, common vowel patterns, compound words, consonant blends, and digraphs correctly.
- spell and use homophones correctly.
- use numbers and abbreviations correctly.
- use resources to find correct spellings.

Getting Started with "Becoming a Better Speller"

Start-Up Activity: Introduce this chapter as a place for students to go when they are proof-reading their written work for spelling errors. Encourage them to use the tips for proofreading on page 308 in the handbook. Consider asking that they make their own check-list of this information and keep it in their writing folders.

Enrichment Activity: Throughout the year, collect writing samples to assess the spelling instruction your students need. As you review your students' work (rough drafts as well as final drafts), note the number of incorrectly spelled words, the types of words that are missed, habitual errors, and so on.

Teaching Resources

Writers Express Teacher's Guide

- Minilessons:

  Grades 4 and 5
  " 'BRrrr' in FeBRuary" (page 244)

Writers Express Handbook

- "Keep a Personal Dictionary," page 293, gives suggestions for keeping a personal list of words and their meanings.

- "Checking Your Spelling," pages 398-401, provides a list of high frequency words.

- "Using the Right Word," pages 402-411, provides a list of homophones and other words that can be confused for one another.

Writers Express Program Guide

- A teaching unit (lesson plans and blackline masters) can be found in the Program Guide ring binder for each grade level.

Giving Speeches

(See handbook pages 311-317.)

Giving a talk, presentation, or formal speech is a skill students will find useful throughout their lives. Whether they find themselves before the student council asking for a new bike rack at school, or before the city council lobbying for a new bike path, students who have some understanding of giving speeches will find public speaking less daunting. This chapter introduces students to the building blocks of speech making.

Rationale

- As students narrow topics for their speeches, they learn to think about an audience and its relationship to their speech's purpose, topic, and tone.
- Learning to give speeches can be a highly enjoyable educational experience.
- Students discover that writing skills and strategies can be used for different purposes. Creating a speech is much like writing a report.

Major Concepts

- **Choosing a speech topic is a personal and thoughtful process.** (page 311)
- **The three main types of speeches are informational, demonstration, and persuasive.** (pages 312-313)
- **The speech-writing process follows the nine steps listed in *Writers Express.*** (pages 312-317)

Performance Standards - - - - -

Students are expected to . . .

- use speaking effectively as a tool for learning, and for communicating a variety of purposes in a variety of settings.
- demonstrate oral presentation skills such as organizing content and adjusting materials for a specific audience.

Getting Started with "Giving Speeches"

Start-Up Activity: In preparation for giving a formal speech, give students informal speaking opportunities. Invite them to make announcements in front of the class—share newsworthy events, tell jokes, or give information. Allow them to use notes.

Enrichment Activity: To give students practice making persuasive speeches, have them choose something they would like to change about their school or neighborhood. Ask them to prepare persuasive speeches that present their ideas and the facts that support them. Encourage students to give their speeches to an appropriate audience, such as the school board, the parent-teacher organization, or a community group.

Teaching Resources

Writers Express Teacher's Guide

- Minilessons:

  Grades 4 and 5
  "Bravo!" (page 244)

Writers Express Handbook

- "Improving Listening Skills," pages 330-331, helps students to become a good audience for classmates' speeches.
- "Taking Good Notes," pages 374-375, offers tips to help students record and learn what they hear.

Writers Express Program Guide

- A teaching unit (lesson plans and blackline masters) can be found in the Program Guide ring binder for each grade level.

Performing Poems

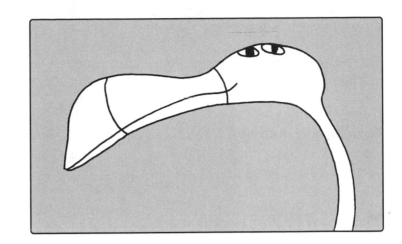

(See handbook pages 318-323.)

Allan Wolf, a senior staff member of "Poetry Alive," loosely defines poetry performance as the process of moving poetry from the page to the stage. Students get on their feet, individually and in teams, to present poetry skits on a stage or at the front of the classroom. The primary concern is with how the poetry is presented rather than with what it is saying. Still, students do have to understand the poetry in order to perform it.

Rationale

- To bring poetry to life, students must read, hear, and speak it.
- By performing, students will understand and relate to poetry in a way not possible through the solitary act of silent reading.
- Performance encourages both participatory and cooperative learning.
- Poetry performance culminates in presentation. This presentation gives students a sense of purpose and accomplishment.
- As students take their performances elsewhere, they learn how to conduct themselves in front of groups.

Major Concepts

- **Because of their sounds and ideas, some poems lend themselves especially well to performance.** (page 318)
- **A five-step process can help students take a poem from page to stage.** (pages 319-323)

Performance Standards - - - -

Students are expected to . . .

- use speaking effectively as a tool for learning, and for communicating a variety of purposes in a variety of settings.
- demonstrate oral presentation skills (organizing content, modulating voice, pacing, using specific techniques purposefully, and adjusting materials for a specific audience).

Getting Started with "Performing Poems"

Start-Up Activity: Have students take turns reading favorite poems aloud. (These may be published or students' poems.) Encourage them to add movements and perhaps background sounds. This will set the stage for performing poems that are scripted and scored.

Enrichment Activity: Art and music projects lend themselves naturally to poetry performance. Students may make masks, costumes, and props for the performance, as well as prepare background music (live or recorded).

Teaching Resources

Writers Express Teacher's Guide

- Minilessons:
  Grade 4
  "Mime Time" (page 244)
  Grade 5
  "Flamingo Flamenco" (page 245)

Writers Express Handbook

- "Writing Poems," pages 239-249, helps students to write the poems, which they may then script and perform.
- "Working in Groups," pages 360-365, presents the skills students need to work together to perform their poems.

Writers Express Program Guide

- A teaching unit (lesson plans and blackline masters) can be found in the Program Guide ring binder for each grade level.

Improving Viewing Skills

(See handbook pages 324-329.)

Television plays a major role in shaping what children know and believe about the world. Most children spend much more time with TV than with their parents. And some kids spend as much time in front of TV as they do in school! That means that children need to be educated viewers of television.

Rationale
- Students need to know how to assess the television programs and commercials that shape their understanding of the world.
- Using viewing guidelines, students will learn more from TV specials.
- Because the World Wide Web is an important new medium, students need to know how to evaluate its content.

Major Concepts
- **Television influences what students know, believe, and buy.** (page 324)
- **Being a critical viewer of TV news means watching for completeness, correctness, and balance.** (page 325)
- **Students can learn more from TV specials by viewing them thoughtfully and actively.** (page 326)
- **Even entertainment programs should be viewed critically.** (page 327)
- **TV commercials use a variety of selling methods to persuade viewers to buy.** (page 328)
- **Like television, the Web is a source of information and entertainment that impacts students' lives.** (page 329)

Performance Standards

Students are expected to . . .
- use effective viewing as a tool for learning.
- interpret media messages (determine stereotypes, biases, and persuasive techniques).

Getting Started with "Improving Viewing Skills"

Start-Up Activity: Have students log their TV-viewing time for one entire week, adding up the number of hours they spent watching TV. As a class, add up the number of hours they spent at school during the same week. Have a discussion about their findings.

Enrichment Activity: Have students, in pairs or small groups, discuss some things they recently bought (or asked their parents to buy) and the factors that influenced those purchases. Did television commercials or programs play a part? Do students feel differently about the products now that they have learned more about TV commercials?

Teaching Resources

Writers Express Teacher's Guide

- Minilessons:

  Grade 4
  "5 W's and H" (page 245)

  Grade 5
  "Be aware." (page 245)

Writers Express Handbook

- "Thinking Clearly," pages 346-349, helps students learn how to evaluate news stories, commercials, and TV specials.

- "Taking Good Notes," pages 374-375, gives tips to help students record and remember what they see.

Writers Express Program Guide

- A teaching unit (lesson plans and blackline masters) can be found in the Program Guide ring binder for each grade level.

Improving Listening Skills

(See handbook pages 330-331.)

Students spend more time listening than they do speaking, reading, and writing combined. With that much "practice," you might expect students to automatically develop good listening skills. But, of course, they don't. With thoughtful practice, however, students can learn how to listen effectively.

Rationale
- Many students are unaware of the difference between hearing and listening.
- Good listening skills help students learn better and faster.
- Good listening skills help students succeed, not only in the classroom but also in their personal relationships and in their lives outside school.

Major Concepts
- **Listening is more than just hearing—it is an active mental process.** (page 330)
- **Good listeners listen with their eyes as well as their ears, and they listen with a good attitude.** (page 331)
- **Active listening entails listening for specific things—main ideas, key words, the speaker's tone of voice, and so on.** (page 331)

Performance Standards

Students are expected to . . .
- use listening effectively as a tool for learning.
- listen for information (follow directions, organize oral information into notes, question for clarification and elaboration).

Getting Started with "Improving Listening Skills"

Start-Up Activity: Have students listen as you describe a favorite place you have visited. Afterward, ask students to draw a detailed picture of the place. (Emphasize that the drawing needn't be perfect, only that it contain all the details mentioned.) To see how well they listened, have students share their pictures. If possible, share a photograph of the place you described.

Enrichment Activity: Play a recording of a familiar song that tells a story. Have students listen carefully, and then write a paragraph about what happens in the "story." Encourage students to include as many details as they can. Share and discuss the students' work.

Teaching Resources

Writers Express Teacher's Guide

- Minilessons:
  Grade 4
  "Telephone" (page 245)
  Grade 5
  "It's a dirty job." (page 245)

Writers Express Handbook

- "Revising with Partners," pages 60-63, offers tips for listening and responding to classmates' writing.
- "Skills for Listening," page 362, helps students to listen actively when working in groups.

Writers Express Program Guide

- A teaching unit (lesson plans and blackline masters) can be found in the Program Guide ring binder for each grade level.

Using Graphic Organizers

(See handbook pages 333-337.)

Graphic organizers are formats (lists, outlines, etc.) and pictures (Venn diagrams) used to frame written ideas. Using graphic organizers will help your students get their thoughts on paper. Once that's accomplished, they can rearrange ideas and rewrite as necessary.

Rationale
- Graphic organizers are excellent tools for organizing and studying information and ideas.
- Students need specific information and advice about how to use graphic organizers.

Major Concepts
- **To be good learners, students must be good thinkers. Knowing how to organize information is an important part of being a good thinker.** (page 333)
- **Different graphic organizers serve different purposes.** (pages 334-336)
- **Observing, gathering, questioning, organizing, imagining, rethinking, and evaluating are helpful strategies for gathering and organizing thoughts.** (page 337)

Performance Standards

Students are expected to . . .
- organize prior knowledge about a topic, including producing a graphic organizer.
- summarize and organize ideas gained from multiple sources in useful forms such as conceptual maps, learning logs, and time lines.

Getting Started with "Using Graphic Organizers"

Start-Up Activity: Together, read aloud a short section from your class science book—one that tells about a cycle, such as the life cycle of an insect or a plant. Have the students make a cycle diagram, using the model on page 282 in the handbook. Discuss the significance of using such a diagram.

Enrichment Activity: Choose a current science or social studies topic. Have students make a gathering grid, writing down the topic, questions they have about it, and sources where they might find answers to their questions. (Refer to pages 46 and 195 in the handbook.) Share and discuss students' work.

Teaching Resources

Writers Express Teacher's Guide

- Minilessons:

  Grade 4
  "Getting It Together" (page 246)

  Grade 5
  "Back to Camp" (page 246)

Writers Express Handbook

- "Gathering Details and Making a Plan," pages 44-49, shows students graphic organizers "at work."

- "Using Reading Strategies," pages 271-276, presents additional organizers for students' use.

Writers Express Program Guide

- A teaching unit (lesson plans and blackline masters) can be found in the Program Guide ring binder for each grade level.

Thinking and Writing

(See handbook pages 338-345.)

Students can't learn to write well until they learn to think well. A vast vocabulary and a flawless command of grammar will result in technically correct nonsense if they aren't thinking clearly.

Rationale
- Students need to be aware that thinking skills are as essential to good writing as mechanics and sentence structure are.
- Students need to learn different ways of thinking and how to use them in their writing.
- Good thinking skills and an awareness of the different kinds of thinking will help students meet challenges both inside and outside the classroom.

Major Concepts
- **Thinking is the foundation for all other classroom skills.** (page 338)
- **Students can, and must, "learn to think."** (page 338)
- **There are six general categories of thinking: recalling, understanding, applying, analyzing, synthesizing, and evaluating.** (pages 339-345)

Performance Standards

Students are expected to . . .
- use effective, logical, and creative thinking skills and strategies.

Getting Started with "Thinking and Writing"

Start-Up Activity: Have students study the guidelines for thinking and writing on page 345. List the six types of thinking on a chart or chalkboard and ask students to recall times they have used them—especially outside of school. This link from the abstract to concrete may help them see the reason for some of their school writing.

Enrichment Activity: Explain that turning a word problem into a math problem takes understanding. Restating something in your own words (or, in the case of a math problem, in symbols) is a good way to show understanding. Give students a word problem. Have them show that they understand the problem by rewriting it as the correct math problem. (Refer to handbook pages 451-453.)

Teaching Resources

Writers Express Teacher's Guide

- Minilessons:

  Grade 4
  "First-Letter Fun" (page 246)

  Grade 5
  "Just the Facts, Ma'am" (page 246)

Writers Express Handbook

- "Thinking Clearly," pages 346-351, offers students more tips for developing their thinking skills.

- "Think of an Argument," page 95, will help students develop and write effective persuasive essays.

Writers Express Program Guide

- A teaching unit (lesson plans and blackline masters) can be found in the Program Guide ring binder for each grade level.

Thinking Clearly

(See handbook pages 346-351.)

As children grow, we ask them to work on organizing their thoughts more clearly. Specific strategies that often involve writing can help students become better thinkers.

Rationale

- Students must learn the difference between facts and opinions.
- When students learn to avoid the pitfalls of fuzzy thinking, they will find it easier to express themselves clearly.
- Students need strategies for making good decisions and solving problems.

Major Concepts

- **An opinion is what someone believes is true. A fact is a statement that can be proven true.** (page 347)
- **"Fuzzy thinking" is a catchall phrase that refers to illogical or misleading statements.** (pages 348-349)
- **Listing and reviewing options are keys to making good decisions.** (page 350)
- **Complicated problems can be solved with a step-by-step plan that involves testing possible solutions.** (page 351)

Performance Standards

Students are expected to . . .
- use effective, logical, and creative thinking skills and strategies.

Getting Started with "Thinking Clearly"

Start-Up Activity: Read aloud an editorial or opinion article from a newspaper or magazine. Ask students to identify the opinions expressed in the article. List them on the board. If the article contains facts that support the opinions, list those, too.

Enrichment Activity: Read aloud a chapter from a novel, a short story, such as a fable, or a narrative poem. Following the reading, ask students for the facts (things that are true) and the opinions (how someone thinks or feels about the facts) found in the piece. List these on the chalkboard and discuss.

Teaching Resources

Writers Express Teacher's Guide

- Minilessons:

  Grades 4 and 5
  "Working It Out" (page 246)

Writers Express Handbook

- The sample "Persuasive Paragraph," page 81, uses facts and opinions to convince someone of something.

- "Writing Persuasive Essays," pages 94-99, offers step-by-step guidelines for a form that requires students to think clearly.

Writers Express Program Guide

- A teaching unit (lesson plans and blackline masters) can be found in the Program Guide ring binder for each grade level.

Writing as a Learning Tool

(See handbook pages 353-355.)

Whether they realize it or not, students who like to write have probably already used writing as a learning tool. Writing can help students figure things out, find and organize their thoughts, and keep in touch with the outside world.

Rationale
- It is important to learn how writing can be used to help order thoughts.
- Students who keep learning logs will improve their comprehension of subject matter.

Major Concepts
- **Writing helps students learn. One important way to write and learn is to keep a learning log.** (page 353)
- **Writing in a learning log is like thinking on paper. Students can record thoughts, feelings, and questions about a subject, as well as new vocabulary words, in their logs.** (page 354)
- **Other ideas for keeping a learning log include first thoughts, stop 'n' write, nutshelling, notes to the teacher, unsent letters, graphic organizers, and drawings.** (page 355)

Performance Standards

Students are expected to . . .
- use writing as a tool for learning.

Getting Started with "Writing as a Learning Tool"

Start-Up Activity: Read and discuss "First Thoughts" and "Notes to the Teacher," handbook page 355. After a class lesson (any subject area), ask students to do one or both of these activities in their learning logs. Discuss the results.

Enrichment Activity: Introduce students to a writing-to-learn strategy called "looping." Have them read a science or social studies assignment and freewrite about it for 2-3 minutes. Then have them look over their freewriting and circle or write down a word or phrase they want to write more about, and freewrite again for 2-3 minutes. Students should repeat the process until they feel they've explored all the important ideas in the reading.

Teaching Resources

Writers Express Teacher's Guide

- Minilessons:
  Grade 4
  " 'I never knew that.' " (page 247)
  Grade 5
  "Get the picture." (page 247)

Writers Express Handbook

- "Writing in Journals," pages 133-137, gives a personal slant to writing and learning.
- "Taking Good Notes," pages 374-375, has tips for improving note-taking skills.

Writers Express Program Guide

- A teaching unit (lesson plans and blackline masters) can be found in the Program Guide ring binder for each grade level.

Completing Assignments

(See handbook pages 356-359.)

Children in the fourth and fifth grades need to manage an ever-increasing number of assignments. This is often a difficult adjustment for them. Many students become frustrated because they aren't sure how to get the job done.

Rationale
- Students can learn specific techniques for setting goals and managing time.
- When students feel in control of their assignments, their confidence grows and their work improves.

Major Concepts
- **How a student learns depends on the student, the teacher, and the texts used.** (page 356)
- **Setting goals involves being realistic, working toward a goal, and rewarding yourself for achieving a goal.** (page 357)
- **Lists and weekly schedules are effective time-management tools.** (page 358)
- **Planning ahead and working in the proper environment are important to successful completion of assignments.** (page 359)

Getting Started with "Completing Assignments"

Start-Up Activity: Have a class discussion about setting goals. Point out that setting and meeting goals boosts self-esteem. Goals needn't be something major, either; planning to get your room cleaned up by the end of the week is an admirable goal. Setting many such smaller goals will increase a student's chance of being successful. Remind students that failing to achieve some goals is not uncommon, and that resetting a goal is perfectly acceptable.

Enrichment Activity: Read aloud a story about someone who has achieved something special. Have students list some goals they think the person might have set in order to achieve that success.

Teaching Resources

Writers Express Teacher's Guide

- Minilessons:

  Grade 4
  "Goal to Go" (page 247)

  Grade 5
  "Sticking to a Schedule" (page 247)

Writers Express Handbook

- "Using Reading Strategies," pages 271-279, provides students with ways to complete their reading assignments effectively and efficiently.

- "Taking Good Notes," pages 374-375, offers tips to increase learning and study skills.

Writers Express Program Guide

- A teaching unit (lesson plans and blackline masters) can be found in the Program Guide ring binder for each grade level.

Working in Groups

(See handbook pages 360-365.)

Students enjoy the opportunity to work with their peers, but teachers often find that the work periods degenerate into unproductive gab sessions. Students can learn to work together productively when they master some basic cooperative learning techniques.

Rationale
- Learning to listen and cooperate can lead to improved performance across the curriculum.
- Learning to work cooperatively is an important life skill.

Major Concepts
- **Listening, cooperating, and clarifying are important "people skills."** (page 360)
- **Planning ahead can help a group stay on task and complete an assignment.** (page 361)
- **To listen effectively, students need to think about what is being said.** (page 362)
- **Cooperating means working with others to reach a shared goal.** (pages 363-364)
- **Clarifying means "clearing up" confusion in group work.** (page 363)
- **Group sharing can be used to discuss books that students have read.** (page 365)

Performance Standards

Students are expected to . . .
- demonstrate discussion skills (retelling, making eye contact, conveying feelings, questioning effectively, leading discussions).
- listen for information (follow directions, organize oral information into notes, question for elaboration and clarification, distinguish between fact and fiction).

Getting Started with "Working in Groups"

Start-Up Activity: Ask students to study a number of U.S. coins in order to find a common element. On all U.S. coins is the motto *E Pluribus Unum* (meaning "out of many, one"). Discuss how this phrase fits our country's identity, and how it also relates to the concept of teamwork.

Enrichment Activity: There are a couple of points in this chapter where students are encouraged to speak up when they don't understand something. As a class, discuss ways for students to ask clear, specific questions that will further their understanding. When a student does speak up in class, ask other students for their input. Often, a student can explain things in a way that another student will comprehend well.

Teaching Resources

Writers Express Teacher's Guide

- Minilessons:
  Grade 4
  "Goin' West" (page 247)
  Grade 5
  "Story Ideas" (page 248)

Writers Express Handbook

- "Revising with Partners," pages 60-63, covers the skills needed in effective writing groups.

- "Improving Listening Skills," pages 330-331, helps students develop one of the most important group skills.

Writers Express Program Guide

- A teaching unit (lesson plans and blackline masters) can be found in the Program Guide ring binder for each grade level.

Taking Tests

(See handbook pages 366-373.)

Students should view tests as a learning tool, not as a gauge of their individual worth. Still, test taking is an unpleasant experience for some students—and a frightening one for others. As everyone knows, though, tests are an inescapable part of school.

Rationale
- Learning how to prepare for and take tests gives students a sense of mastery over this sometimes scary and frustrating part of school.
- Good test-preparation skills help students reinforce what they have learned and learn what they missed the first time around.
- When students know how to prepare for and take tests, their performance more accurately indicates what they have learned.

Major Concepts
- **Test success comes in two stages: *preparing* for the test and *taking* the test.** (page 367)
- **There are two basic kinds of tests: objective and essay. They require different methods of test preparation and test taking.** (pages 368-371)
- **Remembering material is a major key to test success. There are many techniques students can use to improve their recall.** (pages 372-373)

Getting Started with "Taking Tests"

Start-Up Activity: Read aloud a short story or a short nonfiction selection. Then give students two writing prompts, each using a different key word (from page 368 in the handbook). Being certain the students understand the key words, have half the class work with one prompt and the other half work with the other. Share and compare responses from the two groups, noting how the key words guided the answers.

Enrichment Activity: Construct a few objective-test questions on a topic students are studying—testing their understanding of the tips in the handbook. Allow students to refer to the handbook as they take the test.

Teaching Resources

Writers Express Teacher's Guide

*   Minilessons:

    Grade 4
    "Did you say 'test'?" (page 248)

    Grade 5
    "Key Questions" (page 248)

Writers Express Handbook

*   "Writing Expository Essays" and "Writing Persuasive Essays," pages 88-93 and 94-99, provide basic guidelines that will help students respond to writing prompts.

*   "Guidelines for Thinking and Writing," page 345, classifies and explains many of the key words used in essay-test questions.

Writers Express Program Guide

*   A teaching unit (lesson plans and blackline masters) can be found in the Program Guide ring binder for each grade level.

Taking Good Notes

(See handbook pages 374-375.)

Learning how to take good notes is an important skill for students to learn. Writing is a powerful tool for remembering. Requiring students to take notes and then testing them on the material will also encourage them to develop this skill.

Rationale
- Being able to take good notes is an important skill, one students will use more and more throughout their school years.
- Learning to write reflectively broadens students' school experience, enhancing their understanding.

Major Concepts
- **Writing is a powerful learning tool.** (page 374)
- **Note taking means listening carefully and writing down just the important ideas.** (page 374)
- **Three guidelines for improving note-taking skills are *pay attention, be brief*, and *be organized*.** (page 375)

Performance Standards

Students are expected to . . .
- take notes from relevant and authoritative sources such as guest speakers, books, almanacs, encyclopedias, media sources, and articles.

Getting Started with "Taking Good Notes"

Start-Up Activity: Tape-record a short section from a class textbook. Ask students to listen to the recording and take notes, following the guidelines in the handbook. Then have students listen to the recording a second or even a third time, adding to and revising their notes each time. Encourage them to experiment with abbreviations, drawings, graphic organizers, and so on, which can help them quickly record more of the important information in a "real" note-taking situation.

Enrichment Activity: Videotape a segment of an educational program. Have the class watch and take notes. When the video is over, ask volunteers to share their note-taking methods. Also ask for an oral summary of the information presented.

Teaching Resources

Writers Express Teacher's Guide

- Minilessons:
  Grade 4
  "Learning As I Go" (page 248)
  Grade 5
  "Notes on Notes" (page 248)

Writers Express Handbook

- "Using Reading Strategies," pages 271-279, shows additional ways to take effective notes on reading assignments.

- "Improving Viewing Skills," pages 324-329, and "Improving Listening Skills," pages 330-331, help students learn what information should be included in their notes.

Writers Express Program Guide

- A teaching unit (lesson plans and blackline masters) can be found in the Program Guide ring binder for each grade level.

Proofreader's Guide

Introductory Notes

This section introduces the "Proofreader's Guide" in the handbook and provides getting-started ideas to help you with your initial planning.

Proofreader's Guide

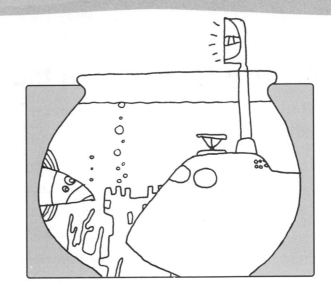

(See handbook pages 376-435.)

Learning the "basic skills" of grammar has relevance for students when these skills are taught in the context of meaningful writing experiences. The "Proofreader's Guide" is the student's handy reference for the information they will need while they are writing and when they are checking their work. These yellow pages are placed near the end of the handbook to demonstrate that the skills of proofreading and editing usually come toward the end of the writing process.

Rationale
- Students need an easy-to-use reference to answer their queries about the standard conventions of language.
- Knowing how to use a reference tool such as the "Proofreader's Guide" is an important learning skill.

Major Concepts
- **"Marking Punctuation" and "Editing for Mechanics" cover the information students need to know about punctuation, capitalization, plurals, abbreviations, and numbers.** (pages 377-397)
- **"Checking Your Spelling" and "Using the Right Word" include high frequency words that students commonly use, and often misspell, in their writing.** (pages 398-411)
- **"Understanding Sentences" and "Understanding Our Language" help students learn about sentences and the parts of speech.** (pages 412-435)

Performance Standards

Students are expected to . . .
- employ standard English to communicate clearly and effectively.
- identify and use the different parts of speech.
- write in complete sentences.
- use punctuation and capitalization correctly.

Getting Started with the "Proofreader's Guide"

Start-Up Activity: Conduct a search, using the following questions about the "Proofreader's Guide." Have students, individually or in pairs, respond to the statements on their own paper.

> **Go to page 376.** Read the table of contents. Then go to the section called "Editing for Mechanics." What kinds of things will you learn about in this section?
>
> **Go to page 417.** Write a single sentence using every part of speech.
>
> **Search pages 398-401.** List five adjectives and five nouns from the spelling list.
>
> **Read about "Subject-Verb Agreement" on page 413.** Write two sentences about the weather. In the first, use a singular subject and a singular verb; in the second, use a plural subject and a plural verb.

Enrichment Activity: Give students an opportunity to demonstrate what they know about punctuation and capitalization. Have them write a dialogue between two students who are talking about a writing assignment (a biographical sketch about a historical figure) that is due at the end of the week.

Teaching Resources

Writers Express Teacher's Guide

- Minilessons:
  Pages 249-259 contain 45 minilessons for the "Proofreader's Guide."

Writers Express Handbook

- "Writing Basic Sentences," pages 113-117, includes a sentence review and information about common sentence errors, sentence agreement, and sentence problems.

Writers Express Program Guide

- SkillsBook activities for all parts of the "Proofreader's Guide" can be found in the Program Guide ring binder for each grade level.

Student Almanac

Introductory Notes

This section introduces the "Student Almanac" in the handbook and provides getting-started ideas to help you with your initial planning.

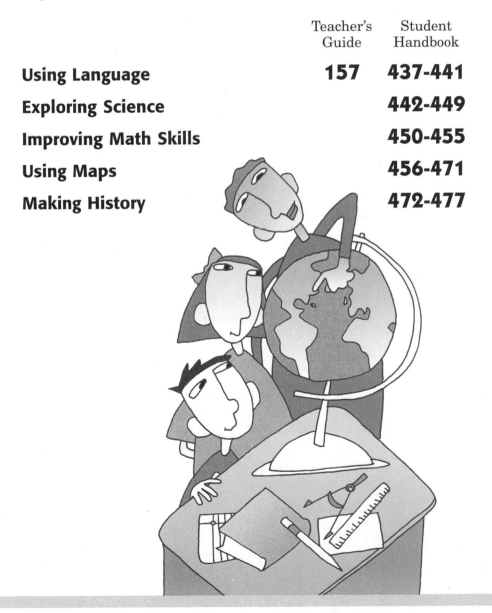

Student Almanac

(See handbook pages 436-487.)

The "Student Almanac" contains a variety of information that students will find useful across the curriculum. This section is divided into five parts: *language, science, mathematics, maps,* and *history.* Students will learn how to use this reference material as they find interesting facts and information.

Rationale
- As students satisfy their natural curiosity about many subjects, they learn how to interpret visual information.
- Students will learn the valuable skill of using reference materials.
- Many of the skills applied to the proper use of language affect other subject areas across the curriculum.

Major Concepts
- **"Using Language" contains information on the history and origins of the English language. It also includes a list of foreign words, as well as the manual and Braille alphabets.** (pages 437-441)
- **In "Exploring Science," students can peruse various tables of scientific information: Animal Facts, Periodic Table of the Elements, Our Solar System, and The Metric System.** (pages 442-449)
- **"Improving Math Skills" offers ways to solve word problems, a list of common math symbols, and a variety of math tables.** (pages 450-455)
- **"Using Maps" explains how to use maps. Students can learn something about the countries of the world.** (pages 456-471)
- **"Making History" takes a close look at the U.S. Constitution, contains a chart of presidents and vice presidents, and includes a historical time line.** (pages 472-487)

Performance Standards - - - - -
Students are expected to . . .
- use reference materials to increase their understanding of a particular subject and expand their knowledge of the relationships between subjects.

Getting Started with the "Student Almanac"

Start-Up Activity: The almanac has five distinct sections: language, science, math, maps, and history. Divide your class into five groups, assigning one of the almanac sections to each group. Ask the groups to study their section and think of interesting and fun ways that they could introduce the information to the class. (You may want to use some of the tips from "Working in Groups," handbook pages 360-365, to help the students get organized.)

Enrichment Activity: Ask students to create a game show or a board game in which all of the questions are based on the content of the "Student Almanac." When the participants play the game(s), they may use their handbooks as a reference.

Teaching Resources

Writers Express Teacher's Guide

- Minilessons:
  Pages 260-262 contain 10 minilessons for the "Student Almanac."

Writers Express Handbook

- "The Tools of Learning," pages 254-375, includes "Working in Groups," pages 360-365, as well as many other learning strategies that students will use across the curriculum.

Writers Express Program Guide

- Blackline masters and minilessons for all parts of the "Student Almanac" can be found in the Program Guide ring binder for each grade level.

Writing Programs

The writing programs described on the following pages offer a variety of approaches to meet the individual needs of your students.

Effective Writing Instruction

So much has been written about writing that it is easy today for any teacher to become overwhelmed by all the different writing approaches. No matter which writing approach you choose, remember that all effective writing instruction shares these two goals:

1. Students learn to write.

Students learn to write in the same way all writers learn—by doing. The best writing program gives students frequent, varied, and significant writing opportunities. Writing isn't taught by teacher lectures, prescriptive textbooks, or isolated skill-and-drill exercises. Students need real purposes and real audiences for their writing. They need constructive, supportive, and challenging responses to their writing, and they need realistic instruction that answers their questions at the time of need.

2. Students write to learn.

Writing is thinking on paper. Writing lets students explore ideas and questions—about themselves, about the world, about subjects they're studying in school. Students in effective writing programs write to understand, learn, discover, clarify thinking, and pass along information.

What are the characteristics of effective writing programs?

Student centered: In strong writing programs, students write rather than listen to a teacher lecture about writing. They experiment with the writing process to discover how writing works for them.

No textbook needed: Most textbooks by their nature are prescriptive. They are designed to teach writing skills, but they are also intended to tie the teacher and student to the textbook. Good writing programs encourage independent thinking and use the students' own writing as the text.

Individualized: Because all writers are unique, one formula for writing doesn't work for all students at the same time. Strong writing programs allow students to write and work individually. The teacher provides assistance and instruction as it is needed.

Interactive classroom structure: Strong writing programs promote active learning. Writing classrooms are structured to reflect real writing experiences. Students interact with each other and with the teacher to discuss their writing. There's no hiding in the last row of the classroom as the teacher lectures.

Adaptable and integrated curriculum: A good writing program is open to improvement. It must be flexible enough to accommodate new methods of writing instruction or assessment. If an existing method or routine doesn't work with a particular group of students, changes are made. In addition, a good writing program combines various approaches to provide the best writing opportunities for the students.

An Overview of the Approaches

As you search for an appropriate writing approach, you will see that these five approaches can be combined. For example, the thematic approach incorporates the process approach and the writing-workshop approach, and could include the trait-based approach. So consider an approach (or a combination) that best fits the needs of your students.

1 Process Approach

While using this approach, students learn that writing—real writing—is a process of exploration and discovery rather than an end product. As students develop their writing, they use all the steps in the writing process—prewriting, drafting, revising, editing and proofreading, and publishing. And the writing they develop, for the most part, stems from their own thinking.

Writers Express discusses the writing process (beginning on page 8). Guidelines for the specific forms of writing are also organized according to the steps in the writing process. (See pages 162-163 in this guide for more on the writing process.)

2 Thematic Approach

When using this approach, the teacher (with student input) chooses a theme that serves as the focal point for an experience that immerses students in a variety of integrated reading, writing, and speaking activities. Writing projects evolve from these activities. (See page 164 in this guide for more on the thematic approach.)

3 Personal Experience Approach

In this approach students enjoy writing and find it meaningful because it stems from their personal experiences and observations.

Both journal writing and freewriting help students write honestly about their personal experiences when they do assigned writing. These types of writing help students produce writing that readers will find interesting and entertaining.

Review the forms of writing in *Writers Express* (pages 40-43). As students become

confident in their personal writing, they become more secure in making their writing public. (See page 165 in this guide for more information.)

4 Trait-Based Approach

Trait-based instruction focuses on key features—or traits—that most writers, editors, and thoughtful readers agree are essential to writing success. A list of these traits follows:

- ✔ stimulating ideas
- ✔ original word choice
- ✔ logical organization
- ✔ smooth sentences
- ✔ personal voice
- ✔ correct, accurate copy

Students are taught each trait individually, but eventually they combine all of them in revising and editing their work. They find examples of each trait in the writing all around them, assessing their own and others' writing for these key features. Trait-based instruction makes writing and revision manageable for students. They may use trait-based rubrics to guide their writing process from start to finish. (See pages 183-188 in this guide for the rubrics and pages 166-167 for more information.)

5 Writing Workshop Approach

In a writing workshop, students write or work on writing-related issues every day (reading, researching, responding, participating in collaborative writing, etc.). They keep all of their writing in folders and produce a specified number of finished pieces each term. They are encouraged to experiment with new forms and techniques. Support during each writing project comes from both peer and teacher conferences. Students use the steps in the writing process to develop their writing, and they share their writing in class.

The teacher acts as a facilitator and guide. Desks and chairs are arranged to make student interaction easy, and the classroom is stocked with relevant reading and writing materials. Instruction and advice are given as they are needed on an individual basis, in small groups, or to the entire class. (See page 168 in this guide for more information.)

The Process Approach

What is the "writing process"?

The process approach emphasizes the steps a student goes through while writing. *Writers Express* divides the writing process into these steps: prewriting, writing, revising, editing and proofreading, and publishing.

Before you begin to implement this approach, remember these key points:

- The writing process is not linear; it is cyclical. Steps or stages are repeated in different orders with different writers and different writing assignments.
- The writing process is unique for every writer.
- Not all writing needs to progress through all the steps of the writing process. Sometimes writing will remain in a prewriting form, and sometimes it will progress through the whole process and become a public piece.

How can the process approach be implemented?

- Provide many models of the writing process in action—professional, student, and your own. Write with your students so that you can work through the writing process with them in real ways.
- Be sure that your students understand and can model the stages of the writing process. In addition, help students individualize the steps of the process to best meet their own writing needs.
- Have students create and use writing folders in which to store writing pieces that are "in progress." Choose a method for organizing the folder. Some teachers use separate folders for each piece of writing; others prefer to put all pieces in one large folder.
- Give students many opportunities for practicing the steps of the writing process—learning the writing process takes time.

> "There is no quick fix for writing a clear sentence . . . Clear writing comes from rereading and revising, not from following strict form."
> —STEPHANIE HARVEY

Strategies for Teaching the Steps in the Writing Process

In addition to the prewriting, drafting, revising, editing and proofreading, and publishing strategies offered in *Writers Express,* try these ideas:

Prewriting

Sensory Clusters

Have students use the cluster with a twist—cluster an idea using the five senses. This is a great way to cluster for a descriptive writing piece.

Question Clusters

Have students cluster focusing on the questions surrounding their topic. Perhaps have them use the 5 W's (who, what, when, where, why, and how) to develop their cluster ideas.

Pros and Cons Freewriting

Help students explore an idea by debating it with themselves. Encourage them to freely write about both the positive and the negative aspects of their topics.

Different Locales Freewriting

When searching for ideas, have students explore different locales, tuning their senses to the possibilities. For example, have them freewrite after taking a walk outside. Ask them to freewrite after visiting a grocery store, a shopping mall, an airport, or a cemetery. The world provides a wealth of writing ideas when it is explored using the senses.

Drafting

Do you hear what I am saying?

Put students into small groups (no more than three students per group). Have them talk through their stories or ideas. Ask them to share with the group and have the others in the group respond. What's clear? What's not?

Great Authors, Great Ideas

Read some great leads and endings to your students. Try to choose very different styles so that your students don't become convinced that there is only one right way to write an introduction or an ending. Choose examples from their favorite authors, read-alouds, and various forms of writing. Read and discuss together what makes each of these introductions and conclusions work.

Collaborative Authors

Practice writing a draft by working collaboratively as a class in developing an idea with a strong beginning, middle, and ending. Plan out the draft and then write it together as a class.

Teacher Drafters

Share your own draft—not a finished product—with your students. Talk with them about how you worked through the drafting process.

Revising

Scaffolding Sections

If a section such as the introduction is giving students problems, invite them to try writing three or four different versions. Do the same for conclusions that are giving them problems. If some part of the middle section is causing problems, try encouraging different ways to include specific details about the topic of the piece.

Teacher Revisers

This activity is a continuation of "Teacher Drafters." Make an overhead of your first draft; discuss the strengths and weaknesses of the draft with your students. Then show your students your revision work and share a second draft.

Editing and Proofreading

Symbol Alert

Share copyediting symbols and practice using them with students.

Post it!

Make posters of particularly effective sentences, and of common usage problems. Post them in the classroom as an inspiration and a reminder for students.

Publishing

Author's Chair

Donald Graves offers the concept of an "author's chair" as an alternative to traditional publishing. Students may take turns sitting in this specially designated chair to share their completed writing pieces as authentic authors.

School Sharing

Have students share their writing with other students in the school. For example, when exploring writing for different audiences, have students write children's stories and then share the final copy with young students.

What are the results of the writing process?

- Students find writing more meaningful because it becomes a reflection of their own thinking.
- Students develop a feel for writing.
- Students develop independent thinking skills and take pride in their work.
- Students develop a better attitude toward writing, which results in better writing for students of all abilities.

The Thematic Approach

What is the thematic approach?

In the thematic approach to writing, students write to respond to literature or to extend what they are learning in another class. To complete writing projects, students may work individually, in small groups, or as a whole class. Other approaches, such as the writing process approach and the writing workshop approach, are often incorporated into the thematic approach.

Before you begin to implement this approach, remember these key points:

- Thematic writing provides an avenue for students to write to learn. Choose a theme that students can explore meaningfully.
- Thematic writing units usually take a week or two to complete. During that time, students work for 30-60 minutes daily on their writing project. They work through the steps of the writing process—from prewriting to publishing.
- Teachers and students work collaboratively on the thematic writing project. While students contribute to decisions about the type of writing project, its length, its audience, and the time schedule, teachers guide them through the writing process.

How can the thematic approach be implemented?

- Students should first be familiar with the theme before beginning a thematic writing project. After students have begun a literature unit, or learned some key concepts in a thematic unit, they will likely be ready to begin.
- Thematic projects may be written individually, in small groups, or as a class. Decide which arrangement works best for the theme, your students, and the type of writing you want them to do.
- The thematic writing approach may incorporate the process approach.

Strategies for Using the Thematic Approach

Prewriting

To introduce the thematic writing project, provide opportunities for students to reflect on the theme. For example, for the theme of aging, ask students to freewrite about their experiences with their grandparents or other elderly people. Read some short stories or a novel about aging, and ask students to record discussions and responses in a writing journal.

Drafting

Collaborate with students to determine an appropriate writing project for the theme. Offering choices helps students take ownership of their writing. For the literary theme of aging, have students write . . .

- a friendly letter to an elderly person,
- a letter to a story character to persuade him or her to take a certain action, or
- a few journal entries as a story character.

Revising

On Your Own ● Use the trait-based approach to have students review and revise their drafts for clear ideas, strong organization, and voice.

Writing Groups ● After self-assessment and revision, have students meet together to share their drafts and discuss possible revisions.

Editing and Proofreading

Red Pen Alert! ● Have students proofread their drafts for correct spelling and punctuation.

Focused Minilessons ● In small groups or with the class, address common problems.

Publishing

Pizzazz and Purpose ● Display writing projects and have a celebration. For example, with the literary theme on aging, consider inviting elderly friends to review the writing projects.

The Personal Experience Approach

What is the personal experience approach?

Personal experience is a natural place for students to begin their writing. With this approach, they explore their thinking, questions, and interests. Developing such personal writing makes students better able to address more complex content-oriented writing later.

Before you begin to implement this approach, remember these key points:

- Journals, which are the main component of the personal approach, can be used in many different ways to accomplish different goals.
- Students are encouraged to write freely in their personal writing journals without worrying about grades.
- The audience for this type of writing is limited—sometimes the writer is the only reader.

How can the personal approach be implemented?

- Establish a classroom environment that invites students to write. Provide stimulating topic ideas through an abundance of resources—books, magazines, posters, displays.
- Write often. Students become more comfortable with writing in journals when they do it often. Establish a weekly routine for journal writing.
- Write for a prescribed period of time. Ask students to write nonstop for 5-10 minutes on a topic. At first this will be difficult, but as students become more comfortable with journal writing, they will be able to write more freely.
- Establish an audience. Will the writing be shared with the teacher? With other students?

Strategies for Implementing the Personal Approach

In addition to the journal-writing strategies provided in the handbook, try these ideas:

Journals for Personal Experiences

The Diary ● In this journal, students record their thoughts. Due to the private nature of this type of writing, it may or may not be shared.

Freewriting Journal ● Teachers direct this journal by offering several prompts that lead students to explore ideas. This journal is used throughout the week for 10-minute quick writes.

Dialogue Journal ● This journal serves as an avenue of communication between teachers and individual student writers. Dialogue may be personal or about a subject area being studied.

Journals for Reactions

Personal Notebook ● In this journal, students record ideas, observations, and insights that they may use in future writing pieces.

Class or Project Journal ● In this journal, students respond to what is being studied in class or what they are reading. Questions, predictions, and commentaries are common in this type of journal. Students also use the class or project journal to record progress in a group project. They document their participation, their responsibilities, and their evaluation of how well their group performs.

Journals for Analyses

Learning Log ● Students use this journal to record what they are learning. In science, for example, this could take the form of an observation log for an experiment. In social studies, this could be a freewriting exploring the relationship between what students are learning now and their past experiences or knowledge. In math, a learning log could explain or summarize the math concepts discussed in class.

The Trait-Based Approach

What is the trait-based approach?

The trait-based writing approach doesn't replace other writing approaches. For example, it may rely on the writing process and the writer's workshop. The focus of the trait-based approach is helping students identify, in their own writing and in the writing of others, those qualities that make writing strong.

Before you begin implementing this approach, remember these key points:

- The trait-based approach helps students develop (a) the skills needed to become good assessors of writing and (b) strategies to improve their writing.
- When students understand the traits of good writing, they can assess their own writing, no matter what form it takes.
- Before you can teach the traits, you need to know them yourself. Check the *Writers Express* handbook for more information on the traits (pages 18-23), as well as the section on assessment in this guide (pages 180-194).

How can the trait-based approach be implemented?

- Teach the traits to students by first identifying and discussing the qualities of good writing. After establishing the criteria that you and your students will use to distinguish good writing, explain how each of the traits focuses on a component of good writing.
- Select writing models from various sources: student pieces (with permission), professional writers, newspaper articles, travel brochures, workplace writing, samples of your own writing. Discuss how the traits of effective writing are (or are not) demonstrated in the models.
- Teach the traits separately, taking as much time as necessary to build student confidence and understanding of each trait. Again, use real models. (See the specific strategies that follow.)

- Have students create posters that illustrate the traits.
- Use trait language when responding to student writing, and ask students to use trait language when responding to one another's writing.
- As a class, with a student's permission, score his or her writing piece together. Keep refining students' assessment skills.
- Encourage peer-response groups (not peer-editing groups) in which students discuss their writing using the traits of effective writing as the standard.
- Share rubrics (scoring guides) with students before they begin writing so they understand your expectations for each writing task.

Strategies for Teaching the Trait-Based Approach

Trait 1: Stimulating Ideas

- Examine a textbook that your students use every day. In small groups, have students find a section that shows good idea development. Share the passage with the class and discuss how it effectively reflects that trait.
- Ask students to bring a paragraph from home—from a newspaper, a recipe, an advertisement. As a class or in small groups, discuss the idea development of each piece.
- Share a model with poor idea development. Then divide students into small groups or assign partners and ask them to improve the poorly developed model so that it reflects strong ideas.

Trait 2: Logical Organization

- Have students give detailed directions from their home to school, or have them explain how to do something. Follow up with a discussion of why clear organization is important.

- Read cookbook directions or how-to manuals to see the importance of careful organization.
- Choose a short story with excellent transitions; cut it up into pieces and have small groups of students reassemble the story. Discuss how transitions aid organization.
- Look at the introductions (and conclusions) of some of your students' favorite read-aloud books. Discuss what makes the introductions and conclusions "work." Have students practice modeling strong introductions and conclusions.

Trait 3: Personal Voice

- Have students freewrite an imaginary conversation with themselves. Suggest a situation such as being alone on a stormy night. Have them write using two different voices—one voice calm and reassuring, the other voice panicked and scared. Share the freewritings and discuss what makes the voices in each of the conversations different.
- Have your students write three sets of recipe directions for the same recipe: one set of directions for a small child, one for an alien from another planet, and one for a classmate. Do this activity in small groups and then share the directions. Discuss how the voice varies depending on the audience.
- Share models of outstanding voice. Ask students to model the professionals.
- Together, define "voice" so that all your students understand the concept. Post the definition along with models demonstrating strong voice on a bulletin board.

Trait 4: Original Word Choice

- Challenge students to find alternatives to overused words. Assign students in small groups to come up with a list of alternatives to a word such as "said" or "nice." Give students a specific time limit and then have them share the words they have chosen as alternatives.
- Make posters of alternative words to keep the choices visible to the students.

- Have some fun with an exaggeration exercise. As an entire class, take a "telling" sentence and add as many descriptions as possible to make it a "showing" sentence. Then split students into small groups and have them create some of their own exaggerated showing sentences.
- Study greeting cards and poetry for examples of carefully chosen words.

Trait 5: Smooth Sentences

- Give students two paragraph models: one with very short, choppy sentences and the other with only one long sentence. Ask students to rewrite the paragraphs by changing the sentence lengths so that sentences in the paragraph flow smoothly from one sentence to the next.
- In small groups, have students choose pages from a favorite novel or lyrics from a song and make a chart of the varying sentence lengths and different sentence beginnings. Challenge them to identify any transitions. Share the results.
- Ask students to read different writing models aloud. Encourage them to read expressively. Discuss how sentence fluency leads to expressive writing.

Trait 6: Correct, Accurate Copy

- Practice editing skills with pages from the *Writers Express SkillsBook*. Students may work on these activities individually, in small groups, or as a class.
- Have students practice editing skills in small groups by focusing on one skill at a time.
- Have students bring in any error examples they find at home—from newspapers, business letters, instructions, etc.
- Reward students for finding your editing errors in classroom handouts!
- Use student-made posters of copyediting symbols in your classroom editing work. (See the inside back cover of *Writers Express* for these symbols.)

The Writing Workshop Approach

What is the writing workshop approach?

The writing workshop approach focuses clearly on a way of structuring writing in the classroom. (See the weekly schedule in the next column.) Before you begin to implement this approach, remember these key points:

- This approach establishes a community of writers. Students and teachers work collaboratively through the writing process.
- The atmosphere of classrooms using the writing workshop approach is relaxed—less structured.
- Students write daily for an established period of time with this approach.
- Students work through the steps of the writing process at their own pace, conferring with other students and the teacher when necessary.

How can the writing workshop approach be implemented?

- Though the classroom structure of this approach is relaxed, routines must be established. Setting up a class schedule allows students to anticipate what they will accomplish within a class period.
- To encourage creative writing topics, stock your classroom with interactive, stimulating resources.
- Establish distinct areas within the classroom for tasks: a conference area, an editing and proofreading area, a writing area, and a publishing area.
- Establish your role as facilitator of the writing process. Your role is not to provide topic ideas for students, but to respond to, discuss, develop, encourage, and even challenge writing ideas provided by students.

Strategies for Implementing the Writing Workshop Approach

See a writing workshop in action by studying the sample schedule below. Here you will see how one teacher organized his writing workshop. This schedule reserves time for minilessons, status checks, individual or group work, and sharing sessions.

Because the schedule is designed for one of the first weeks of a workshop, all students are asked to participate in the minilessons. In time, you can meet the needs of your students by inviting only those attempting certain goals or encountering particular problems to do minilessons. All other students will be actively engaged with a piece of writing or another option you have offered.

Mon.	Tues.	Wed.	Thurs.	Fri.
Writing Minilessons (10 minutes as needed)				
Status Checks (2 minutes) Find out what students will work on for the day.				
Individual Work (30 minutes) Writing, Revising, Editing, Conferencing, or Publishing				
Whole Class Sharing Session (5 minutes)				

Writing Throughout the Day

The strategies and guidelines discussed in this section will help your students use writing as an important learning tool in the content area, whether it is mathematics, science, or language arts.

Introduction to Writing Across the Curriculum

> "Writing every day, students get an opportunity to work out rules and patterns of spelling and grammar, to experiment with language, to try out new genres, and to explore topics and ideas."
>
> **—REGIE ROUTMAN**

Writing across the curriculum (WAC) is the use of writing as a teaching and learning tool in all subject areas. Based on subject matter and learning goals, each teacher chooses which writing activities to use and how to use them. The following pages provide specific ways to implement different forms of writing in a WAC program.

Getting Started with Writing Across the Curriculum

Before you implement this approach, remember these key points:

- Writing-across-the-curriculum activities can take many forms: graded and nongraded, short and long, school-based and personal, writing that's revised and edited and writing that isn't.

- Writing-across-the-curriculum activities not only help students write to learn, but also help students learn to write.

- Writing across the curriculum helps teachers achieve their content and learning goals through appropriate writing activities.

Guidelines for Implementing Writing Across the Curriculum

As you prepare to implement writing across the curriculum, identify your learning goals and objectives in a particular subject area. Then consider legitimate reasons to use writing assignments in your classroom based on your goals and objectives. Five common reasons are illustrated below:

1 **Writing to share learning** lets students interact with an audience and builds a healthy learning community. Common forms of writing assigned for this purpose are traditional classroom writing forms. Naturally, these forms can be, and are often, used in subject areas other than English. Guidelines and models of many different writing forms are listed below.

Classroom Writing Forms:	*Writers Express* handbook pages
* biographies	151-155
* book reviews	166-170
* classroom reports	192-203
* descriptions	100-105
* expository essays	88-93
* how-to writing	172-175
* feature stories	156-163
* multimedia computer reports	204-207
* newspaper stories	156-163
* observation reports	188-191
* paragraphs	75-87
* persuasive essays	94-99
* plays	232-237
* poetry	239-253
* stories from history	226-231
* summaries	185-187

2 **Writing to show learning** is the most popular reason why teachers have students write in courses other than English. *Writers Express* provides many writing forms that allow students to show what they have learned.

Classroom Writing Forms:	*Writers Express* handbook pages
* book reviews	166-170
* classroom reports	192-203
* essay tests	368-369
* multimedia computer reports	204-207
* observation reports	188-191
* summaries	185-187

3 **Writing to understand new concepts and ideas** is another good reason to write. Teachers who want students to write for this purpose often assign forms of writing-to-learn activities. Below are several writing forms that help students understand new concepts and ideas.

Classroom Writing Forms:	*Writers Express* handbook pages
* comparison/contrast essays	92-93
* descriptive writing	100-105
* how-to writing	172-175
* learning logs	353-354
* prewriting activities brainstorming, clustering, focused writing, listing	35-36
* request letters	176-179
* writing-to-learn activities	355

4 **Writing to explore personal thoughts and feelings** helps students connect with any topic in any class. Students can discover what they know and what they are confused about by using the writing forms listed below.

Classroom Writing Forms:	*Writers Express* handbook pages
* friendly notes and letters	144-146
* journals	134-137
* learning logs	353-354
* letters of complaint	180
* letters to the editor	157, 164-165
* narrative writing	106-111
* personal narratives	138-143
* poems	239-253
* social notes	148-149

5 **Writing to think through and complete classroom tasks** helps students finish projects and meet deadlines. Some writing forms, like explanations, help students organize their ideas in order to complete work more effectively. Below are guidelines and models for several writing forms that can help students complete classroom tasks.

Classroom Writing Forms:	*Writers Express* handbook pages
* e-mail	147, 266
* explanations	172-175
* journals	
—response	171
—dialogue	136-137
—personal	134-135
* memos	182-183
* note taking	374-375
* request letters	176-179

Strategies for Using Writing Across the Curriculum

Writing-to-Learn Activities

- prove appropriate in all subject areas
- require no preparation or prewriting
- enhance class discussions
- sharpen listening skills when read aloud to the class
- need no revising
- need not be graded
- usually are not revised
- work as prewriting activities (See pages 36-38 in *Writers Express*.)

Admit Slips: Admit slips are brief pieces of writing (usually fit on half sheets of paper) that can be collected as "admission" to class. Admit slips can call for a summary of yesterday's class work, a list of questions about class material, a request for the teacher to review particular ideas, or anything else students may have on their minds. The teacher can read several aloud (without naming the writers) to help students focus on the day's lesson.

Brainstorming: Brainstorming is done for the purpose of collecting as many ideas as possible on a particular topic. Students will come away with ideas that might be used to develop a writing or discussion topic. In brainstorming, everything is written down, even if it seems to be weak or irrelevant.

Clustering: Clustering begins with students placing a key word in the center of the page and circling the word. They then record other words related to this word. Each word is circled, and a line is drawn to connect it to the closest related word. This is a helpful planning tool.

Completions: Students complete an open-ended sentence (provided by other students or the teacher) in as many ways as possible. Writing completions can help students look at a subject in different ways or encourages them to focus their thinking on a particular concept.

Correspondence: One of the most valuable benefits of writing to learn is that it provides many opportunities for students to communicate with their teachers and classmates. Teachers should set up a channel (mailboxes, suggestion boxes, special reply notes, memos, e-mail, etc.) that encourages students to communicate freely and honestly.

Creative Definitions: Students are first asked to write out definitions for new words. Other students are then asked to figure out whether each definition is fact or fiction. When students are given the actual definition, there is a much better chance they will remember it.

Dialogues: Students create an imaginary dialogue between themselves and a character (a public or historical figure, or a character from literature). The dialogue brings to life information being studied about the subject.

Dramatic Scenarios: Students are asked to imagine themselves to be historical characters during key moments in these people's lives, and then write dialogues that capture the moment.

Exit Slips: At the end of class, students write a sentence or two in which they summarize, evaluate, or question something about the day's lesson, and then turn in their exit slips. Teachers use the exit slips to assess students' learning or the success of a lesson.

Focused Writings (Freewriting): Writers select a single topic (or one part of a topic) and write nonstop for a time. Like brainstorming, focused writing allows students to see how much they have to say on a particular topic, as well as how they might go about saying it.

How-To Writing: To help them clarify and remember information about a task, students write instructions or directions on how to perform the task. Ideally, they then test their writing on someone who is unfamiliar with the task.

Learning Logs: A learning log is a journal in which students keep their notes, thoughts, and personal reactions to a subject being studied. (See handbook pages 353-355.)

Listing: With listing, students begin with any idea related to the subject and simply list all the thoughts and details that come to mind. Listing can be useful as a quick review or progress check.

Predicting: Students are stopped at a key point in a lesson and asked to write what they think will happen next. This works especially well with lessons that have a strong cause-and-effect relationship.

Question of the Day: Writers are asked to respond to a question ("What if?" or "Why?") that is important to a clear understanding of the lesson. To promote class discussion, the writing is usually read aloud.

Student Teachers: Students construct their own math word problems and discussion questions (which can be used for reviewing or testing). This writing task is a great way to replace routine end-of-the-chapter or workbook questions with questions that students actually wonder about or feel are worth asking.

Summing Up: Students are asked to sum up what was covered in a particular lesson by writing about its importance, a possible result, a next step, or a general impression left with them.

Warm-Ups: Students can be asked to write for the first 5 minutes of class. The writing can be a question of the day, a freewriting, a focused writing, or any other writing-to-learn activity that is appropriate. Warm-ups help students focus on the lesson at hand.

Practical Writing Forms

Practical Writing Activities

- help students complete work in all classes
- facilitate tasks that are part of extracurricular activities
- serve as part of a larger unit or project
- use guidelines and models in *Writers Express*
- require revising and polishing
- are usually collected and graded

While each form has an assignment for a specific subject, these forms of writing can be used anywhere. (Page numbers refer to guidelines and models in *Writers Express*.)

Business Letter (pages 176-181)
Mathematics: Write a business letter to a local carpenter. Ask how a knowledge of math helps him or her on the job.

E-mail (pages 147 and 266)
Social Studies: Send an e-mail to your senator or a member of Congress, giving your opinion about a current event or issue.

Explanation (pages 172-175)
Science: Explain how to work like a scientist. List the steps of the scientific method studied in class.

Feature Article (pages 159-163)
Physical Education: Write a feature article about one of your classmates. Interview your classmate and share his or her interests and unique abilities in your classroom newspaper.

Journals (pages 133-137)
Art, Science, History, Math, Music: Use your classroom journal to keep track of the progress you are making on an extended project.

Memo (pages 182-183)
Language Arts: Send a memo to your group members to remind them of the props they need to bring for your play.

Request Letter (page 179)
Social Studies: Send a letter of request to ask for brochures, pamphlets, or other types of information for a topic being researched.

Classroom Writing Forms

Classroom Writing Activities

- include the traditional forms of writing taught in school
- are commonly introduced in English class
- form a basis for learning course material in all classes
- are collected and graded
- serve as one part of a unit or project
- use guidelines and models shown in *Writers Express*

While each form has an assignment for a specific subject, these forms of writing can be used in any subject area. (The page numbers refer to guidelines and models in *Writers Express*.)

Autobiography (pages 138-143)
Social Studies: Write a brief autobiographical essay about your family's holiday traditions.

Biography (pages 151-155)
Art: Write a biographical sketch of an artist you've studied in class.

Book Review (pages 166-171)
Science: Write a review of a book written about one of your favorite science topics.

Classroom Report (pages 192-203)
Social Studies: Research and write a report about an invention that has made your life easier or more pleasant.

Description (pages 100-105)
Geography: Write a descriptive paragraph or essay about an interesting land formation.

Essay Test (pages 368-369)
Music: Compare and contrast woodwind instruments to brass instruments. Support your answers with specific details.

Expository Essay (pages 88-93)
Social Studies: Write an essay explaining the history and meaning of your state flag.

Explanation (pages 172-175)
Health: Explain how the heart pumps blood throughout your body.

Feature Story (pages 156-163)
Music: Write a feature article about a musician in your community.

Historical Story (pages 226-231)
Social Studies: After studying the early colonies of America, write a story about a nine-year-old child traveling from England to America by ship.

Journal (pages 133-137)
Science: For one week, keep track of all the different birds you see in your neighborhood. Try to identify them by name or draw sketches of the birds you see.

Learning Log (pages 353-355)
Mathematics: At the end of each week, write an entry in your learning log that explains the math concepts you learned during that week. Try to explain them in as much detail as possible. Try to see ways these concepts could apply to your life.

Multimedia Computer Report (204-207)
Science: Create a report about the life cycle of frogs.

News Story (pages 156-163)
Social Studies: Write a news story as a reporter interviewing a person whose actions or thoughts changed people's lives.

Note Taking (pages 374-375)
Music: In your class notes, draw and label the instruments in the school band.

Observation Report (pages 188-191)
Science: Write an observation report on the growth of a bean from seed to small plant.

Persuasive Essay (pages 94-99)
Science: Write a persuasive essay about why your school should have a recycling program.

Play (pages 232-237)
Science: Write a play that dramatizes an interesting scientific discovery.

Poetry (pages 239-249)
Science: After studying about light and how it is refracted, write a poem about rainbows.

Summary (pages 185-187)
Health: Write a summary of your textbook's explanation of the digestive system.

Writing for Specific Subject Areas

The activities that follow are designed for one of seven specific subject areas—science, mathematics, social studies, health/physical education, music/art, geography, and language arts. They are the kinds of activities that are usually revised and polished by the students and collected and graded by the teacher. Each activity can be tied to guidelines and models in *Writers Express*.

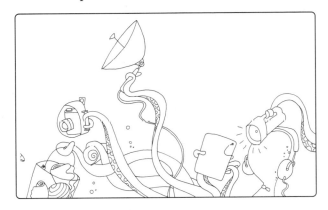

SCIENCE

- **Biome Biography** Research a particular animal from the biome that you've studied. For example, after a study of grasslands and deserts, research coyotes, prairie dogs, rattlesnakes, roadrunners, bison, or quail. Write a classroom report based on your research. (See "Writing a Classroom Report," pp. 192-203.)

- **Blast Off!** Write a feature article or news story about a famous astronaut or space mission. (See "Writing Newspaper Stories," pp. 156-163.)

- **Walking Tour** Take a walk around your neighborhood and observe the different types of trees and plants. Collect some leaves from them, and write an observation report that describes the trees and plants in detail. (See "Writing Observation Reports," pp. 188-191.)

- **Weather Watchers** Interview a local weather forecaster. Learn how weather is observed, measured, and predicted by professionals. Share your findings through a feature article. (See "Writing Newspaper Stories," pp. 156-163.)

MATHEMATICS

- **What's the word?** Create a math dictionary defining and explaining math concepts that you are currently studying in math class. (See "Keep a Personal Dictionary" page 293.)

- **Story Problems** Create a short story about a student who needs to take a train from Chicago to New York. Based on the story, create story problems about train schedules and lost luggage. Exchange the problems with classmates and solve each other's problems. (See "Writing Realistic Stories," pp. 220-225.)

- **How did you do that?** Write a how-to paragraph explaining how to do long division. (See "How-To Writing," pp. 172-175.)

- **Rain, Rain, Go Away!** Keep track of the rainfall amounts for one month and then create a graph using graphing skills learned in math class. Include this graph in a multimedia computer report about your state. (See "Multimedia Computer Reports," pp. 204-207.)

SOCIAL STUDIES

- **Hear Ye, Hear Ye!** Write and deliver a speech that an explorer such as Lewis or Clark would give to his companions before setting off on an expedition. (See "Giving Speeches," pp. 311-317.)

- **Powwow** After studying a unit on Native American history, write a dialogue between you and an important Native American leader. (See "Writing in Journals," pp. 133-137.)

- **Gold Digger** Write a fictional story about the lives of two young friends in a California mining camp during the gold rush. (See "Writing Stories from History," pp. 226-231.)

- **Fan Club** Research or interview a person who has an occupation that interests you. Share your findings in a biographical sketch. (See "Biographical Writing," pp. 151-155.)

HEALTH/PHYSICAL EDUCATION

- **Pyramid Power** For one week, record in your journal all the foods you eat. At the end of the week, chart how those foods fit in the food pyramid and record whether you are receiving the daily requirements of each food group. (See "Writing in Journals," pp. 133-137.)

- **Young Olympians** Research and write a biographical sketch about one of your favorite Olympic athletes. (See "Biographical Writing," pp. 151-155.)

- **Please Visit** Write a letter inviting a local doctor, chiropractor, or physical therapist to make a presentation to your class about maintaining healthy bodies. (See "Writing a Business Letter," pp. 177-181.)

MUSIC/ART

- **Art Gallery** After viewing a classroom "gallery" of paintings, choose one and write a descriptive paragraph or essay about it. Without mentioning the title or artist, describe the painting in as much detail as possible. Read the description aloud, and let your classmates guess which painting is being described. Then hang your description next to the appropriate painting. (See "Descriptive Writing," pp. 100-105.)

- **Painting Poetry** Write a poem about one of the paintings displayed in your school. Express how that painting makes you feel or what it makes you think about. (See "Writing Poems," pp. 239-249.)

- **Creating with Papier-Mâché** Write "how-to" directions for making and using papier-mâché. (See "How-To Writing," pp. 172-175.)

- **I wish I were a . . .** Write a fictional story from the perspective of one of the lesser-known instruments in a band or an orchestra—for example, the tuba, cello, or triangle. (See "Writing Fantasies," pp. 209-215.)

- **Hold the Applause** Write a feature article about a famous composer or an artist you are studying in class. (See "Writing Newspaper Stories," pp. 156-163.)

GEOGRAPHY

- **Presenting . . .** Create an advertisement or a multimedia computer presentation urging people to visit your state. Include information about land, resources, and climate. (See "Multimedia Computer Reports," pp. 204-207.)

- **A View from Above** Write a poem about someone's view of your community from an airplane. (See "Writing Poems," pp. 239-249.)

- **Turn Left Here** Write directions from your home to the school and share them with classmates by having them trace the path on a posted map. (See "How-To Writing," pp. 172-175.)

LANGUAGE ARTS

- **Dear . . . ,** Write a letter from one character in a novel or short story to another, discussing a problem related to the story. (See "Friendly Notes and Letters," pp. 144-146.)

- **Book Poetry** Instead of a traditional book report, write a poem related to a novel or short story. The poem should express the main ideas of the book or explore the relationships of the characters. (See "Writing Poems," pp. 239-249.)

- **Here I Am** Create a silhouette outline of your head on black construction paper. Use this silhouette as a background for a poem or an autobiographical sketch about yourself. (See "Writing Poems," pp. 239-249, and "Writing Personal Narratives," pp. 138-143.)

- **Travel the World** Write a travel brochure based on the setting of a novel or short story studied in class. Be sure to point out several reasons to visit this place and describe its attractions in great detail. (See "Descriptive Writing," pp. 100-105, and "Writing Persuasive Essays," pp. 94-99.)

Designing a Writing Assignment

Students rarely take off on writing assignments—not willingly at least—unless the work seems worth the effort. One way to show the work's value is to design meaningful course objectives, connect the assignment to the objectives, and evaluate the assignment with related criteria. When students see that doing an assignment helps them achieve something valuable, the task seems worth the effort.

Listed on this page are four subject areas: social studies, science, mathematics, and language arts. Beneath each subject you will find (1) one of the subject's objectives, (2) a writing assignment that addresses the objective, and (3) evaluation criteria that writers can use to refine their writing.

SOCIAL STUDIES

Social Studies Objective: To learn how hurricanes form and what effects they can have on coastal communities.

Assignment: For the past few weeks, we have been studying weather conditions such as hurricanes. Based on your knowledge of hurricanes, create a fictional hurricane and write a news story about what happened when it struck land. Remember to include details such as where and when the hurricane struck, how people prepared for the hurricane, what kinds of weather conditions the hurricane produced, and how people responded after the hurricane was over. Use your knowledge of hurricanes to write a believable, detailed news story.

Evaluation: Does the news story describe accurately what happened before, during, and after the hurricane and demonstrate the student's understanding of hurricanes?

SCIENCE

Science Objective: To learn how high and low sounds are made.

Assignment: After this unit about sound, write in your science journal your predictions and observations as we conduct an experiment with rubber bands stretched over the opening of a cigar box. First write your predictions based on your knowledge of sound, and then record your observations as we do the following: What happens to the sound when the rubber bands are tightened and then plucked? What happens to the sound when we pluck thick rubber bands compared to thin rubber bands? Compare the cigar box with its rubber bands, to other musical instruments.

Evaluation: Does the journal entry clearly show the student's understanding of sound and an ability to apply that knowledge to different instruments and different situations?

MATHEMATICS

Mathematics Objective: To learn to make change for any amount up to $1.00.

Assignment: After completing exercises and drills on making change, write a short story or play about a trip to the mall. Include many situations that require the shopper to purchase items and receive correct change.

Evaluation: Does the story or play clearly demonstrate the student's ability to make change correctly and apply the math knowledge to real-life decision making?

LANGUAGE ARTS

Language Arts Objective: To communicate sincerely with older relatives and friends.

Assignment: After a literature unit focusing on the theme of aging, write a free-verse poem about an older relative or friend whom you love and respect. Focus on what you have learned or might learn from this person.

Evaluation: Does the poem demonstrate the student's appreciation for an elderly person and illustrate an awareness of the opportunity to learn from older people?

Designing Your Own Assignments

Subject:

Audience:

Purpose:

Form of Writing:

Prewriting Activities: (Prewriting activities are important, especially if the assignment does not grow out of information or concepts already covered in class.)

1.

2.

Evaluation Guidelines: (Include appropriate checklists and guidelines from *Writers Express*.)

1.

2.

3.

4.

Assessment Strategies and Rubrics

The information in this section covers a number of areas related to assessing students' writing, including using assessment as a teaching tool, using peer assessment, and using writing portfolios.

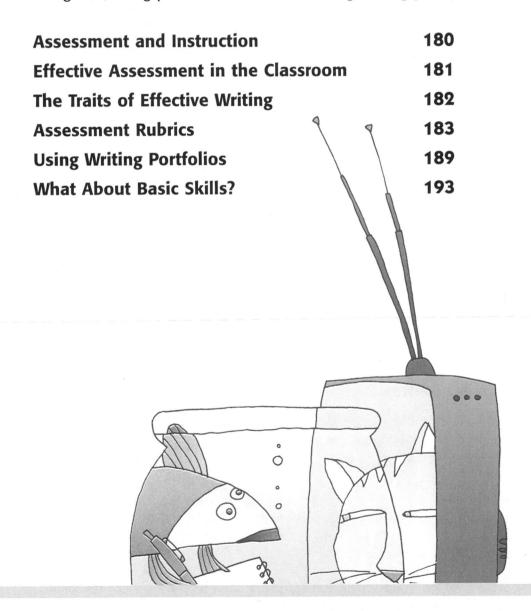

An Overview—Assessment and Instruction

> "Unless we show children how to read their writing, their work will not improve."
>
> **—DONALD GRAVES**

In the past, writing assessment was almost always held to be the province of the teacher. Students turned in work—then waited to see what grades they would receive. Now it is widely recognized that learning to be a good assessor is one of the best ways to become a strong writer. In order to assess well, students must learn to recognize good writing. They must know and be able to describe the difference between writing that works and writing that does not work. Students learn to assess by going through three key steps:

1. Learning about the traits of writing by which their work—and that of others—will be assessed

2. Applying the traits to a wide variety of written texts

3. Applying the traits to their own work—first assessing it for strengths and weaknesses, and then revising it as needed

Why should students be assessors?

Students who learn to be assessors also . . .

■ learn to think like writers,

■ take responsibility for their own revising, and

■ make meaningful changes in their writing—instead of simply recopying a draft to make it look neater.

Role of Teachers and Students

Here is a quick summary of the kinds of activities teachers and students usually engage in while acting as assessors in the classroom.

Teachers

As assessors, teachers who match their assessment to instruction engage in . . .

■ roving conferences, roaming the classroom, observing students' work, and offering comments or questions that will help take students to next steps.

■ one-on-one conferences, in which students are asked to come prepared with a question they need answered.

■ informal comments—written or oral—in which the teacher offers a personal response or poses a reader's question.

■ reading student work, using a general *assessment rubric* such as the ones in this guide (pages 184-188).

■ tracking scores over time to calculate a final grade for a grading period.

Students

As assessors, students often engage in . . .

■ reviewing evaluation guides such as the checklist on handbook page 23 or on page 190 in this guide or the rubrics in this guide on pages 184-188.

■ using a *peer response sheet* such as the one on handbook page 63 or on page 191 in this guide.

■ assessing and discussing written work that the teacher shares with the class.

■ assessing their own work, using a checklist or rubric.

■ compiling a portfolio and reflecting on the written work included.

Effective Assessment in the Classroom

> "Good assessment starts with a vision of success."
>
> —RICK STIGGINS

Good assessment helps students see how they are growing as writers. It indicates to teachers which students are finding success, as well as the specific kinds of help other students may need. To ensure that assessment is working in your classroom, you should do the following things:

- Make sure all students know the criteria you will use to assess their writing. If you are going to use a rubric, provide them with copies.

- Send home copies of rubrics or checklists to parents, too, so they can help their children know what is expected of them.

- Make sure your instruction and assessment match. You cannot teach one thing and assess students on another—if you expect them to be successful.

- Involve students regularly in assessing . . .
  - ✔ published work from a variety of sources,
  - ✔ your work (share your writing—even if it's in unfinished draft form), and
  - ✔ their own work.

- Don't grade *everything* students write, or you'll be overwhelmed with stacks and stacks of papers to assess. Instead, you should encourage students to write *often*; then choose a few pieces to grade.

- Respond to the content *first*. Then look at the conventions. Correctness is important, but if you comment on spelling and mechanics before content, the message to the student is, "I don't care as much about what you think and say as I do about whether you spell everything correctly."

- Encourage students to save rough drafts and to collect pieces of work regularly in a portfolio. This type of collection helps students see how they are progressing as writers.

- Keep your written comments in the margins of student papers. Comments on sticky notes can be even less obtrusive.

Conducting Conferences

Conduct conferences to keep communication lines open with student writers at all points during the development of a piece of writing. Here are three common practices that you can use to communicate with student writers during a writing project:

- **Desk-Side Conferences** occur when you stop at a student's desk to ask questions and make responses. Questions should be open-ended. This gives the writer "space" to talk and clarify his or her own thinking about the writing.

- **Scheduled Conferences** give you and a student a chance to meet in a more structured setting. In such a conference, a student may have a specific problem or need to discuss or simply want you to assess his or her progress on a particular piece of writing.

Note: A typical conference should last from 3 to 5 minutes. Always try to praise one thing, ask an appropriate question, and offer one or two suggestions.

- **Small-Group Conferences** give three to five students who are at the same stage of the writing process or are experiencing the same problem a chance to meet with you. The goal of such conferences is twofold: first, to help students improve their writing and, second, to help them develop as evaluators of writing.

The Traits of Effective Writing

> "Students are more engaged when indicators of success are clearly spelled out."
>
> **—JUDITH ZORFASS & HARRIET COPEL**

Most students could list the traits of a good friend (loyal, kind, good listener) or the traits of a good taco (meat, lettuce, lots of cheese), but could they list the qualities of good writing? As a teacher, it's your job to help students first identify these qualities, or traits, and then learn how to use and talk about the traits in reference to their own writing.

How do the "traits" connect to assessment?

Traits are qualities or characteristics that define strong performance in writing. These traits can be summarized in checklists, rubrics, or scoring guides that define performance along a continuum.

Learning to be a good assessor is one of the best ways for students to become strong writers. Students must know and be able to describe the traits that exemplify writing that works and writing that does not work. Students learn to assess, generally, by going through three key steps:

1. Learning about the traits of writing that will be used to assess their work

2. Applying the traits to a wide variety of written texts

3. Applying the traits to their own work—first assessing it for strengths and weaknesses and then revising it as needed

What traits are important to writing?

When teachers across the country are asked to identify and define what they value in good writing, the traits listed below are most often mentioned.

Stimulating Ideas

Good writing includes a clear, focused, well-defined topic or thesis and all the details needed to bring the topic to life.

Logical Organization

Good writing contains a strong lead or "hook," sequencing that makes sense, transitions that link ideas together, and a powerful wrap-up or conclusion.

Personal Voice

The best writing contains the personal imprint of the writer, together with clear enthusiasm for the topic and concern for the informational needs and interests of the audience.

Original Word Choice

Good writing demonstrates the writer's skills in finding that "just right" word or phrase that makes meaning clear and reading a pleasure.

Smooth Sentences

Good writing flows smoothly from one sentence to the next. Sentences are strong, well crafted, and varied.

Correct, Accurate Copy

Good writing reflects the writer's careful attention to conventions such as spelling, punctuation, grammar, and capitalization. For more on traits of effective writing, see *Writers Express,* pages 18-23.

Assessment Rubrics

This section includes rubrics to assess the following modes of writing: *narrative, expository, persuasive, report,* and *responding to literature.* Use these rubrics as indicated below:

Narrative Writing

Use this rubric with story writing and forms of autobiographical and biographical writing that recall specific events. (See page 184.)

Expository Writing

Use this rubric with informational writing, including expository essays, summaries, basic paragraphs, feature articles, workplace writing, etc. (See page 185.)

Persuasive Writing

Use this rubric with persuasive essays, book reviews, editorials, etc. (See page 186.)

Report Writing

Use this rubric with classroom reports and personal research reports. (See page 187.)

Responding to Literature

Use this rubric when responding to short stories, fables, plays, tall tales, poems, and so on. (See page 188.)

What is a rubric?

A rubric is simply a list of criteria by which a piece of writing may be assessed. It should include a list of traits or qualities that demonstrate what makes a particular piece of writing effective. Students should always know beforehand what criteria will be used to assess their writing.

How do I use the rubrics to score writing?

The rubrics list the traits of effective writing as explained in the handbook (the same traits used to assess writing on many state writing assessment tests).

Each rubric is based on a 5-point scale. A score of 5 means that the writing strongly addresses a particular trait. A score of 3 means that the writing is average or competent, and a score of 1 means that the writing is incomplete or needs more development. Remember: A piece of writing does not necessarily have to exhibit all of the descriptors under each trait to be effective.

The rubrics may be used to assess a work in progress as well as final drafts, and may be modified to meet the needs of the students or the writing being assessed.

Do not combine and average the scores on the rubric to come up with an overall score and then give this score to the student. Seeing their scores for each trait will allow students to see where they need to improve and also where their strengths lie. It is critical that students have an opportunity to assess their own work and then make changes and revisions *before* it is marked with a final score or grade.

After students have completed their revisions and it is time for you to assess their final efforts, remember to respond to content first and then conventions. You may want to make some comments about each paper as a whole on sticky notes or at the end of the work.

How can I use the rubrics as a teaching tool?

Ask students to evaluate a piece of writing using a rubric as a guide. At first, you may have students focus on just one specific trait (like *ideas* or *organization*). Later on, they can evaluate a selection for all of the traits. The more they practice evaluation, the more comfortable they will become with this "writer's language" and begin to exhibit the traits in their own writing.

ASSESSMENT RUBRIC

Narrative Writing

Narrative writing tells a story. The best narratives have a point to make, often in the form of a problem to solve or a challenge to overcome. Personal narratives are stories from the writer's memory. Creative (fictional) stories include a plot, a setting, and a set of characters.

_____ **STIMULATING IDEAS**
- The writer creates an experience for readers.
- The writing solves an important problem or conflict.

_____ **LOGICAL ORGANIZATION**
- The beginning of the story invites readers to read on.
- The sequence of events in the story makes sense.
- All events relate to the main conflict or problem or experience.
- The story ends in a memorable or satisfying way.

_____ **PERSONAL VOICE**
- The writing reveals the writer's (or characters') thoughts and feelings.
- The writing holds the attention of readers.

_____ **ORIGINAL WORD CHOICE**
- The writing has powerful action verbs and colorful description.
- The dialogue, if used, adds life to the story.

_____ **SMOOTH SENTENCES**
- The story is easy to read.
- The writing has a variety of sentence beginnings and lengths.

_____ **CORRECT, ACCURATE COPY**
- The writing is free of most errors in grammar, punctuation, and spelling.
- The paper is neat and ready for sharing.

Scoring Guide

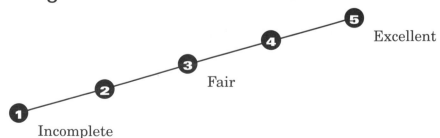

(Add comments on the back of this sheet or at the bottom of the student's paper.)

Expository Writing

Expository writing should answer a question about a particular subject (What's it like to travel in China? Why do poodles make good pets?). Sometimes expository writing is based on formal research; other times, it is based on personal experience and observation. The topic sentence (or main idea) must be supported by facts, comparisons, or quotations from reliable sources.

_____ **STIMULATING IDEAS**
- The writing has a clear focus or main idea.
- The writing has accurate, interesting details that support the main idea.

_____ **LOGICAL ORGANIZATION**
- The writing has a strong beginning.
- Each paragraph includes details that support its topic sentence.
- The writing ends with a clear conclusion about the subject.

_____ **PERSONAL VOICE**
- The writing holds the attention of readers.
- The writing shows the writer's interest in the subject.

_____ **ORIGINAL WORD CHOICE**
- The writing contains specific nouns and verbs and descriptive modifiers.
- The writing defines terms that the readers need to know.

_____ **SMOOTH SENTENCES**
- The writing is easy to read.
- The writing has a variety of sentence beginnings and lengths.

_____ **CORRECT, ACCURATE COPY**
- The writing is free of most errors in grammar, punctuation, and spelling.
- The paper is neat and ready for sharing.

Scoring Guide

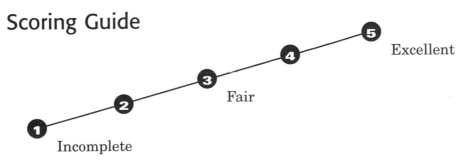

5 — Excellent
4
3 — Fair
2
1 — Incomplete

(Add comments on the back of this sheet or at the bottom of the student's paper.)

ASSESSMENT RUBRIC

Persuasive Writing

Persuasive writing is meant to convince the reader to see things the way the writer does and agree with the writer's position on an issue. It must clearly state the writer's position, support any opinion with evidence, and present these facts in an organized way. It may also challenge the reader to take action.

_____ **STIMULATING IDEAS**

- The writing clearly states the writer's viewpoint or opinion.
- Evidence (facts, details, and examples) supports the writer's opinion.

_____ **LOGICAL ORGANIZATION**

- The opening shares the writer's opinion.
- Each paragraph covers reasons why the writer holds this opinion, and the facts are arranged logically.
- The conclusion summarizes important details.

_____ **PERSONAL VOICE**

- The writing shows that the writer feels strongly about the topic.
- The viewpoint remains the same throughout the writing.

_____ **ORIGINAL WORD CHOICE**

- The writing contains strong words to persuade the reader.

_____ **SMOOTH SENTENCES**

- The ideas flow smoothly, making the writing easy to read.
- The writing includes a variety of sentence beginnings and lengths.

_____ **CORRECT, ACCURATE COPY**

- The writing is free of most errors in grammar, punctuation, and spelling.
- The paper is neat and ready for sharing.

Scoring Guide

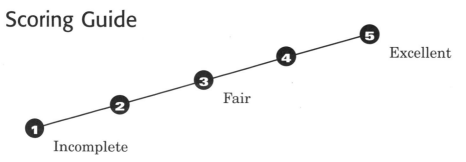

5 Excellent
4
3 Fair
2
1 Incomplete

(Add comments on the back of this sheet or at the bottom of the student's paper.)

Report Writing

A report, like expository writing, is meant to inform. However, in a report, students are asked to first select a topic and then collect information from several sources. Finally, they synthesize this information into a cohesive, well-written paper.

_____ **STIMULATING IDEAS**

- The writing has a clear main idea or topic.
- The writing includes specific facts and details, especially those that are unusual or not commonly known about the subject.

_____ **LOGICAL ORGANIZATION**

- The report has a beginning, a middle, and an ending.
- All of the details are about the subject.

_____ **PERSONAL VOICE**

- The writer sounds like he or she is knowledgeable about the subject.
- Interesting facts and details make the report memorable.

_____ **ORIGINAL WORD CHOICE**

- All words are used correctly.
- The writing explains new words related to the subject.

_____ **SMOOTH SENTENCES**

- The writing has a variety of sentence beginnings and lengths.
- The ideas flow smoothly from one to another, making the writing easy to read.

_____ **CORRECT, ACCURATE COPY**

- The report is free of most errors in grammar, spelling, capitalization, and punctuation.
- The paper is neat and ready for sharing.

Scoring Guide

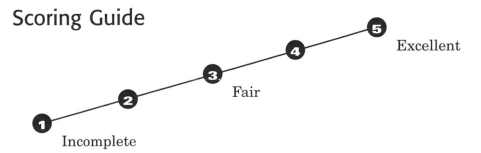

5 — Excellent
4
3 — Fair
2
1 — Incomplete

(Add comments on the back of this sheet or at the bottom of the student's paper.)

ASSESSMENT RUBRIC

Responding to Literature

In writing about literature, students demonstrate their understanding of what they have read. Telling what they liked or did not like about a selection helps students to think creatively and critically. Encouraging others to read a particular selection helps students learn to write persuasively.

_____ **STIMULATING IDEAS**

- The writing answers three questions: What is the selection about? Why do I like (or not like) it? What message or important ideas did the author share?
- The writing covers important elements of the reading selection.

_____ **LOGICAL ORGANIZATION**

- The beginning of the writing pulls readers in.
- The conclusion helps readers know whether they want to read the selection.

_____ **PERSONAL VOICE**

- The writing shows enthusiasm for the selection.
- The writing shows an understanding of the selection, often by showing how it was memorable.

_____ **ORIGINAL WORD CHOICE**

- The writing uses words that make the subject come alive.

_____ **SMOOTH SENTENCES**

- The writing has a variety of sentence beginnings and lengths.
- The writing is easy to read and sounds good when read aloud.

_____ **CORRECT, ACCURATE COPY**

- Proper attention is given to spelling, capitalization, and punctuation.
- Titles of published works are properly punctuated.
- The paper is neat and ready for sharing.

Scoring Guide

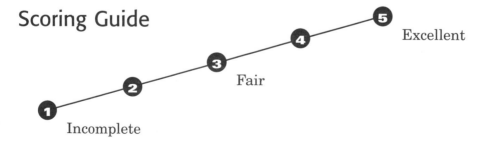

5 Excellent
4
3
Fair
2
1
Incomplete

(Add comments on the back of this sheet or at the bottom of the student's paper.)

Using Writing Portfolios

Many teachers are making portfolios an important part of their writing programs. Will portfolios work for you? Will they help you and your students assess their writing? Read on and find out.

What is a writing portfolio?

A writing portfolio is a collection of a student's writing for evaluation. A portfolio is different from the traditional writing folder. A writing folder (also known as a working folder) contains *all* of a student's work; a portfolio contains only selected pieces.

There are two basic types of portfolios. A *showcase portfolio* is usually presented for evaluation at the end of a grading period. As the name implies, it should contain a selection of a student's best work. A *growth portfolio* notes the way in which a writer is changing and growing. This type of portfolio is usually collected regularly—say, once a month—throughout the year. (See pages 30-33 in the handbook for more information.)

Why should students compile portfolios?

Having students compile writing portfolios makes the whole process of writing more meaningful to them. They will more willingly put forth their best efforts as they work on various writing projects, knowing that they are accountable for producing a certain number of finished pieces. They will more thoughtfully approach writing as a recursive process of drafting, sharing, and rewriting, knowing that this process leads to more effective writing. And they will more carefully polish finished pieces (for showcase portfolios), since their final evaluation will depend on the finished writing they include in their portfolios.

How many pieces of writing should be included in a portfolio?

Although you and your students will best be able to decide this, we advise that students compile at least two to three pieces of writing in a showcase portfolio each quarter. (The number of pieces in a growth portfolio may vary from month to month.) All of the drafts should be included for each piece. Students should also be expected to include a reflective writing or self-critique sheet that assesses their writing progress. (See page 192.)

When do portfolios work best?

Students need class time to work on writing if they are going to produce effective portfolios. If they are used correctly, portfolios turn beginning writers into practicing writers who need regularly scheduled blocks of time to "practice" their craft, to think, talk, and explore options in their writing. (See page 192.)

How can I help my students with their portfolio writing?

Have students explore topics of real interest to them. Also allow them to write for different purposes and audiences and in many different forms. Schedule sharing sessions.

In addition, expect students to evaluate their own writing and the writing of their peers as it develops. Pages 190-192 include the following blackline masters:
- Traits of Good Writing Checklist
- Partner Response Sheet (peer assessment)
- Writing Reflection (portfolio self-evaluation)

How do I grade a portfolio?

Base each grade or assessment on goals you and your students establish beforehand and on what is achieved in the portfolio. Many teachers develop a critique sheet for assessment based on the goals established by the class. An overall assessment honors the students' efforts. Consider (1) quality of content, (2) effective presentation, and (3) thoughtful self-reflection.

Traits of Good Writing Checklist

Directions This checklist will help you use and assess the traits of good writing.

✔ **Stimulating Ideas**

___ Did I present important, interesting information?

___ Did I hold the reader's attention all the way through?

✔ **Logical Organization**

___ Did I include a clear beginning, middle, and ending?

___ Did I use specific details to support the main ideas?

✔ **Personal Voice**

___ Did I show my enthusiasm for the topic?

___ Is my writing easy to read aloud or listen to?

✔ **Original Word Choice**

___ Did I use strong verbs, specific nouns, and colorful adjectives?

___ Did I help the reader picture what I am writing about?

✔ **Smooth Sentences**

___ Did I mix short sentences with longer ones?

___ Did I show variety in my sentence beginnings?

✔ **Correct, Accurate Copy**

___ Did I follow the basic rules of spelling, capitalization, grammar, and punctuation?

___ Is my paper neatly formatted?

Hint: **For helpful checklists on revising and editing, see page 194 in this guide and pages 57, 63, and 67 in your handbook.**

Partner Response Sheet

Revising

Directions Ask a partner to use this sheet to help you revise your writing.

Response Sheet

● I noticed these strong parts in your writing . . .

● I liked this part of your writing . . .

● Here's an idea to make your writing better . . .

Writing Reflection

Title: _____ Date: _____

I chose to put this piece of writing in my portfolio because

_____

_____

_____

_____

As I worked on this piece, I learned _____

_____

_____

_____

In my future writing, I would like to _____

_____

_____

_____

_____

What About Basic Skills?

Research indicates that the study of grammar apart from a writing context has no real impact on writing quality (except for the implementation of the types of activities listed on this page).

Of course, students need some basic understanding of grammar and mechanics to produce accurate final drafts of papers.

Student writers can find the help they need in a handy guide to the rules of grammar and usage (such as the "Proofreader's Guide" in the *Writers Express* handbook).

How can I promote meaningful grammar instruction?

The following types of activities or procedures will help students gain a better understanding of grammar and mechanics:

- Link grammar work as much as possible to the students' own writing.

- First, note the problem. Don't make a big issue of it. Simply make it clear to the student what the problem is and why it is a problem.

- Then refer the student to the pages in the handbook about commas, so he or she can see how to correct the problem.

- Also have the student keep track of this error in a special section of a notebook or a writing folder, so he or she will know what to look for the next time a piece of writing must be edited and proofread.

- If the problem demands special attention, or it is common to many students in the class, teach a direct lesson on the skill or assign a related minilesson or skillsheet. (See pages 225-262 in this guide for minilessons.)

- Make editing of the students' writing an important part of classroom work. They should practice editing and proofreading cooperatively prior to grading. (See the blackline master on page 194.)

- Use minilessons for grammar instruction rather than hour-long grammar activities. (See pages 249-262 in this guide.)

- Remind students that you expect them to watch for this problem in future writing.

- Assess those conventions you have taught.

- Immerse students in all aspects of language learning: reading, writing, speaking, listening, and thinking. Educator James Moffett says the standard dialect is "most effectively mastered through imitating speech."

- Ask students to correct only pieces that go through the entire writing process; it's not necessary to correct or assess practice drafts of all writing assignments or journal entries.

- Don't overwhelm students with too much grammar too often. Find out which skills give your students problems and focus your instruction accordingly.

- You may want to keep a poster-sized list of frequently misspelled words displayed in the classroom. Hold students responsible for spelling these words correctly.

What approaches can I use?

Sentence combining: Use the students' own writing as much as possible. The reasoning behind combining ideas and the proper punctuation for combining should be stressed.

Sentence expansion and revising: Give students practice adding and changing information in sentences that they have already created. Let them expand and revise one another's writing.

Sentence transforming: Have students change sentences from one form to another (from passive to active, beginning a sentence in a different way, and so on).

Sentence imitation: Students should practice imitating writing models. According to James Moffett, this activity teaches grammar as it exposes young writers to the many possibilities of English grammar beyond the basic forms. (See handbook page 128 for guidelines and models.)

Editing and Proofreading Checklist

Directions Use this checklist when you edit and proofread your writing.

✔ Sentence Fluency

___ Did I write clear and complete sentences?

___ Did I write sentences of different lengths?

___ Did I begin my sentences in different ways?

✔ Word Choice and Usage

___ Did I use powerful verbs, specific nouns, and colorful modifiers?

___ Did I use the correct word (*to, too,* or *two*)?
(**SEE** handbook pages 402-411.)

___ Did I use subjects and verbs that agree in number?
(**SEE** handbook pages 116 and 413.)

✔ Punctuation

___ Did I end sentences with correct punctuation marks?

___ Did I use commas in a series (*Larry, Moe, and Curly*)?

___ Did I place commas before coordinating conjunctions (*and, but, or, so, yet*) in compound sentences?

___ Did I punctuate dialogue correctly?
(**SEE** handbook pages 378, 379, and 386.)

✔ Capitalization

___ Did I start each of my sentences with a capital letter?

___ Did I capitalize the names of specific people, places, and things?

✔ Spelling

___ Did I check for spelling errors, including the ones my computer spell checker could have missed?
(**SEE** handbook pages 398-401.)

Reading Strategies

The strategies on the following pages will help you promote personalized, active reading in your classroom.

Insights into Skillful Reading

"Good readers self-monitor, search for cues, discover new things about text, check one source of information against another, confirm their reading, self-correct when necessary, and solve new words using multiple sources of information."

—IRENE C. FOUNTAS AND GAY SU PINNELL

Listed below are the types of insights that critical readers gain over time through their reading experiences. Sharing these insights with students may help them become more insightful and skillful readers themselves.

Short Fiction

- Studying the characters helps readers connect with a story.
- Point of view—the vantage point from which a story is told—controls how much readers will learn about each character.
- Knowing the basic structure of a plot leads to understanding a story.
- The description of the setting contributes to the mood in a story.
- Connecting a story's theme or message to their own lives helps readers find deeper meaning in a story.

Poetry

- Studying the sensory details in a poem leads to a better understanding of the poet's message or purpose.
- Exploring figures of speech deepens readers' insights into a poem.
- Studying a poem's rhymes and rhythms helps readers appreciate its "music."
- Responding personally to a poem leads to better understanding.
- Noting the sound patterns—alliteration, repetition, etc.—gives readers insights into the power of figurative language.

Nonfiction

- Using a reading strategy (such as "think and read") connects readers more thoughtfully to a text. (See handbook page 272.)
- Sorting out the main ideas and supporting details is the basis for understanding nonfiction texts.
- Making generalizations based on the reading leads to better understanding.
- Considering causes and effects helps readers connect ideas as they read.

Persuasive Writing

- Identifying the writer's viewpoint is the starting point for understanding a persuasive piece.
- Knowing that persuasive writers may use loaded words and stories that appeal to the emotions helps readers judge the quality of an author's argument.

Authors

- Writers draw on experiences and relationships in their own lives to create believable characters and situations in their stories.
- Writers of historical fiction blend events that happened in history with fictional details to make history come alive.
- Writers tackle tough issues to show that there are lessons to be learned from difficult situations.
- Writers use exaggeration to entertain and add humor and to give insights into the characters and their actions.

Themes

- Readers may ask themselves "What is the writer trying to say to me?" while reading. They will know the theme when they can answer that question.
- Readers can look for additional themes beyond the primary one. These secondary themes can add to their understanding and appreciation of a text.

Responding to Literature

When students respond to something they have read, they are creating meaning. The responses can be written, oral, or hands-on projects.

Written Responses

Write a letter related to the book.

- Write a letter to a character in the book, telling him or her why you would like to be a friend.
- Send a letter to the author of the book, asking some questions and expressing your feelings about the book.
- Send a letter to the publisher of the book to find out if there will be more books on the topic, or if the book you read will have a sequel.

Write a poem related to the book.

- Write a traditional poem such as a ballad, cinquain, or limerick about a character, an episode, a setting, or an idea.
- Create a playful poem (list, concrete, or name) about a character, an episode, a setting, or an idea.

Write creatively.

- Do a make-believe interview of a character from the book. Create some questions and then write the answers the way you think the character would answer.
- Write a feature article (for a newspaper) about one of the characters.
- Pretend you are a character in the book. Write a five-page diary entry for your character.

Respond in literature logs.

- Complete phrases like *I noticed . . . , I loved the way . . . , I wonder about . . . , What if . . . , It seems like . . . , I was surprised . . . .*
- As you are reading, write questions for your teacher, the author, or another reader.

Oral Responses

Work in a group.

- Get together with others who have read the book. Plan and perform an improvisational skit or a pantomime of a favorite scene.
- Read a special part aloud. Use a section with dialogue or write a dialogue to present as reader's theater.
- Have a literature discussion with three other students.

Work alone.

- Give a book talk. Include an oral summary of the book and reasons why others should read it.
- Do an interpretive reading of a favorite section.

Projects as Responses

Use technology.

- Do a multimedia presentation of important parts or ideas from the book.
- Tape-record several of your favorite parts of the book. Tell why these are your favorite parts. Add sound effects if you'd like.

Use art.

- Make a collage of words and pictures related to the story or topic of the book.
- Illustrate a favorite scene or an idea you learned from the book.
- Draw one or two of the characters from the book. Use the author's description(s).
- Design a new cover for the book.

Reading for Pleasure

> "Reading is a special opportunity [for students] to engage the emotions and thoughts foremost in their minds."
>
> **—DAVID BLEICH**

Experiencing Literature

Reading can be an extraordinary delight. You can help your students discover this for themselves.

Students need an opportunity to read for pleasure. They need to be allowed to lose themselves in a book or other pieces of writing without being asked for a response or formal evaluation.

They must have time . . . time to discover all the worlds and feelings and people who live between the covers of books. They must have time and space to experience reading because, according to Regie Routman, reading is inspiration and sustenance for the imagination, the heart, and the soul!

When you set aside class time for pleasure reading, you should model for them the pleasure of reading. This is not a time to correct papers or catch up on paperwork from the front office.

Reading for pleasure means reducing the rules to the bare minimum. Allow students to abandon a book or read two or three books simultaneously. And, allow them to share their thoughts and feelings about their reading.

The following four rules should be all that is required for pleasure reading to work in your classroom:

1. Have a book in hand when it is time for pleasure reading to begin.
2. Read for the entire time.
3. Do not work on homework.
4. Do not talk or disturb others.

Pleasure Reading in Action

Here are three effective, pleasurable reading activities for you and your students to try.

People still love to hear a book read.
When you read to your students, you are showing them how to give voice to characters, how to let feelings flow, how to interpret a book. When you read aloud to your students, you are giving them something to share together. Sharing a book is a pleasurable way for teachers and students to really get to know each other.

Literature conversations are small-group discussions of a book. The main focus of this activity is a common book that students can enjoy talking about, questioning, and reflecting on. Some simple guidelines for literature conversations can be found in "Sharing Books," page 365 in the handbook.

Here are some specific tips:

1. Listen carefully to one another and write down your reactions and questions.
2. Add to what the others say about a book.
3. Share your personal thoughts about the book, too.

Chew! is another effective activity—a very peaceful, satisfying way to spend a lunch hour. Students arrive with both a lunch to eat and a book to read.

Reading-Writing Lists

The Process of Writing

The Better Brown Stories
Allan Ahlberg, 1995

Life Riddles
Melrose Cooper, 1993

My Name Is Maria Isabel
Alma Flor Ada, 1993

One Brave Summer
Ann Turner, 1995

Riffraff
Judith Clarke, 1992

Rope Burn
Jan Siebold, 1998

Step-by-Step Making Books
Charlotte Stowell, 1994

Utterly Yours, Booker Jones
Betsey Duffey, 1995

Write Up a Storm with the Polk Street School
Patricia Reilly Giff, 1993.

Writing in Journals

Arthur, for the Very First Time
Patricia MacLachlan, 1980

Birdie's Lighthouse
Deborah Hopkinson, 1997

Cassie Binegar
Patricia MacLachlan, 1982

Celia's Island Journal
Celia Thaxter (adapted by Loretta Krupinski), 1992

Chasing After Annie
Marjorie Weinman Sharmat, 1981

Dear Mr. Henshaw
Beverly Cleary, 1983

Double Acts
Jacqueline Wilson, 1998

The Great Railroad Race: The Diary of Libby West, 1868
Kristiana Gregory, 1999

Hey World, Here I Am!
Jean Little, 1989

I'm in Charge of Celebrations
Byrd Baylor, 1986

The Journal of Joshua Loper: A Black Cowboy
Walter Dean Myers, 1999

Linnea's Almanac
Christina Bjork, 1989

Mostly Michael
Robert Kimmel Smith, 1987

Mr. and Mrs. Thief
Naomi Kojima, 1980

My Heart Is on the Ground: The Diary of Nannie Little Rose, a Sioux Girl
Ann Rinaldi, 1999

Sister
Eloise Greenfield, 1974

Speaking of Journals: Children's Book Writers Talk About Their Diaries, Notebooks and Sketchbooks
Paula Graham, 1999

Zlata's Diary: A Child's Life in Sarajevo
Zlata Filipovic, 1994

Writing Personal Narratives

All-of-a-Kind Family
Sydney Taylor, 1951

Astrid Lindgren: Storyteller to the World
Johanna Hurwitz, 1989

Bigmama's
Donald Crews, 1991

Bill Peet: An Autobiography
Bill Peet, 1989

A Bookworm Who Hatched
Verna Aardema, 1992

The Case of the Elevator Duck
Polly Berends, 1989

Celebrating Families
Rosmarie Hausherr, 1997

Childtimes: A Three-Generation Memoir
Eloise Greenfield and Lessie Jones Little, 1993

Don't You Know There's a War On?
James Stevenson, 1992

A Drawing in the Sand: A Story of African American Art
Jerry Butler, 1998

Families: A Celebration of Diversity, Commitment, and Love
Aylette Jenness, 1990

Firetalking
Patricia Polacco, 1994

A Forever Family
Roslyn Banish, with Jennifer Jordan-Wong, 1992

Writing Personal Narratives *(continued)*

Go and Catch a Flying Fish
Mary Stolz, 1991

A Grain of Wheat
Clyde Robert Bulla, 1985

Homesick: My Own Story
Jean Fritz, 1982

The Hundred-Penny Box
Sharon Bell Mathis, 1975

I'm in Charge of Celebrations
Byrd Baylor, 1986

I'm the Big Sister Now
Michelle Emmert, 1989

Journey
Patricia MacLachlan, 1991

Journey to Jo'burg: A South African Story
Beverley Naidoo, 1986

L'Chaim: The Story of a Russian Emigre Boy
Tricia Brown, 1994

Little by Little: A Writer's Education
Jean Little, 1987

A Long Way from Chicago: A Novel in Stories
Richard Peck, 1998

Looking Back: A Book of Memories
Lois Lowry, 1998

The Moon and I
Betsy Byars, 1992

The Moon Lady
Amy Tan, 1992

Mr. Ape
Dick King-Smith, 1998

Nana Upstairs and Nana Downstairs
Tomie dePaola, 1978

Once Upon a Time
Eve Bunting, 1995

Our Journey from Tibet: Based on a True Story
Laurie Dolphin, 1997

Owl Moon
Jane Yolen, 1987

Portrait of a Farm Family
Raymond Bial, 1995

Pueblo Storyteller
Diane Hoyt-Goldsmith, 1991

The Relatives Came
Cynthia Rylant, 1993

The Remembering Box
Eth Clifford, 1985

Second Cousins
Virginia Hamilton, 1998

Snowdrops for Cousin Ruth
Susan Katz, 1998

Song and Dance Man
Karen Ackerman, 1988

Song of the Trees
Mildred Taylor, 1975

Stars Come Out Within
Jean Little, 1990

The Stories Huey Tells
Ann Cameron, 1995

War Boy: A Country Childhood
Michael Foreman, 1990

When I Was Young in the Mountains
Cynthia Rylant, 1985

Where the Flame Trees Bloom
Alma Flor Ada, 1994

The Window
Michael Dorris, 1997

Friendly Notes and Letters

At Her Majesty's Request: An African Princess in Victorian England
Walter Dean Myers, 1999

Beethoven Lives Upstairs
Barbara Nichol, 1994

Dear Annie
Judith Caseley, 1991

Dear Brother
Frank Asch, 1992

Dear Dad, Love Laurie
Susan Beth Pfeffer, 1989

Dear Dr. Bell . . . Your Friend, Helen Keller
Judith St. George, 1992

Dear Emily
Maureen Stewart, 1986

Dear Mr. Henshaw
Beverly Cleary, 1983

Dear Mrs. Parks: A Dialogue with Today's Youth
Rosa Parks and Gregory J. Reed, 1996

Dear Napoleon, I Know You're Dead But . . .
Elvira Woodruff, 1992

Dearest Grandmama
Catherine Brighton, 1991

A Letter to Amy
Ezra Jack Keats, 1968

Letters of Thanks
Manghanita Kempadoo, 1969

Love from Your Friend, Hannah
Mindy Warshaw Skolsky, 1998

Mailbox Quailbox
Margaret Ronay Legum, 1985

Sarah, Plain and Tall
Patricia MacLachlan, 1985

Your Best Friend, Kate
Pat Brisson, 1989

Biographical Writing

All for the Better: A Story of El Barrio
Nicholasa Mohr, 1993

Anne Frank
Rachel Epstein, 1997

Arctic Explorer: The Story of Matthew Henson
Jeri Ferris, 1989

Around the World in a Hundred Years: From Henry the Navigator to Magellan
Jean Fritz, 1994

Christopher Columbus: How He Did It
Charlotte and David Yue, 1992

The Country Artist: A Story About Beatrix Potter
David R. Collins, 1989

The Dalai Lama
Demi, 1998

Dare to Dream: Coretta Scott King and the Civil Rights Movement
Angela Shelf Medearis, 1994

Ezra Jack Keats: A Biography with Illustrations
Dean Engel and Florence B. Freedman, 1995

A Fairy-Tale Life: A Story About Hans Christian Andersen
Joann J. Burch, 1994

Farmworker's Friend: The Story of Cesar Chavez
David R. Collins, 1996

Fine Print: A Story About Johann Gutenberg
Joann J. Burch, 1991

George Washington Carver: Nature's Trailblazer
Teresa Rogers, 1992

Getting the Real Story: Nellie Bly and Ida B. Wells
Sue Davidson, 1992

Helen Keller: Toward the Light
Steward and Polly Graff, 1992

I Have a Dream
Jim Haskins, 1992

John Muir: Wilderness Protector
Ginger Wadsworth, 1992

Katie Henio: Navajo Sheepherder
Peggy Thomson, 1995

Laura Ingalls Wilder: Storyteller of the Prairie
Ginger Wadsworth, 1997

Listening to Crickets: A Story About Rachel Carson
Candice Ransom, 1993

The Look-It-Up Book of Presidents
Wyatt Blassingame, 1990

Margaret, Frank, and Andy: Three Writers' Stories
Cynthia Rylant, 1996

Mark Twain! A Story About Samuel Clemens
David R. Collins, 1994

The Picture History of Great Inventors
Gillian Clements, 1994

The Real Johnny Appleseed
Laurie Lawlor, 1995

Sacagawea
Judith St. George, 1997

Squanto, Friend of the Pilgrims
Clyde Robert Bulla, 1990

Starry Messenger
Peter Sis, 1996

Susie King Taylor: Destined to Be Free
Denise Jordan, 1994

Up in the Air: The Story of Bessie Coleman
Philip S. Hart, 1996

What's the Big Idea, Ben Franklin?
Jean Fritz, 1996

Will You Sign Here, John Hancock?
Jean Fritz, 1997

Wilma Mankiller
Linda Lowery, 1996

Young Frederick Douglass: The Slave Who Learned to Read
Linda Walvoord Girard, 1994

The Young Life of Mother Teresa of Calcutta
Claire J. Mohan, 1996

Writing Newspaper Stories

Extra! Extra! The Who, What, Where, When and Why of Newspapers
Linda Granfield, 1994

Princess of the Press: The Story of Ida B. Wells-Barnett
Angela Medearis, 1997

The Young Journalist's Book: How to Write and Produce Our Own Newspaper
Donna Guthrie, 1998

Writing Book Reviews

Arthur, for the Very First Time
Patricia MacLachlan, 1980

Bridge to Terabithia
Katherine Paterson, 1977

Mariah Delany's Author-of-the-Month Club
Sheila Greenwald, 1990

Shipwreck at the Bottom of the World
Jennifer Armstrong, 1998

How-To Writing

Click! Fun with Photography
Susanna Price and Tim Stephens, 1997

Crafts for Kids: 50 Great Reasons to Get Your Hands Dirty
Diane Rhoades, 1995

Farmer Boy
Laura Ingalls Wilder, 1971

Freckle Juice
Judy Blume, 1978

Hatchet
Gary Paulsen, 1988

The Kids' Multicultural Cookbook: Food and Fun Around the World
Deanna F. Cook, 1995

Little House in the Big Woods
Laura Ingalls Wilder, 1953

The Mash and Smash Cookbook: Fun and Yummy Recipes Every Kid Can Make!
Marian Buck-Murray, 1997

The Most Excellent Book of How to Be a Clown
Catherine Perkins, 1996

The New Way Things Work
David Macauley, 1998

Soda Poppery
Stephen Tchudi, 1986

Trouble River
Betsy Byars, 1989

Why Does the Cat Do That?
Susan Bonners, 1998

Business Writing

Better Than a Lemonade Stand! Small Business Ideas for Kids
Daryl Bernstein, 1992

The Kid's Address Book: Over 3,000 Addresses of Celebrities, Athletes, Entertainers and More . . . Just for Kids
Michael Levine, 1997

Messages in the Mailbox: How to Write a Letter
Loreen Leedy, 1991

Writing Observation Reports

Apache Rodeo
Diane Hoyt-Goldsmith, 1995

Autumn Across America
Seymour Simon, 1993

Backyard Bird Watching for Kids
George H. Harrison, 1997

Barrio: Jose's Neighborhood
George Ancona, 1998

Bridges to Change: How Kids Live on a South Carolina Sea Island
Kathleen Krull, 1995

Buffalo Days
Diane Hoyt-Goldsmith, 1997

Cowboys: Roundup on an American Ranch
Joan Anderson, 1996

Fiesta Fireworks
George Ancona, 1998

Kodoma: Children of Japan
Susan Kuklin, 1995

Kofi and His Magic
Maya Angelou, 1996

Konnichiwa! I Am a Japanese-American Girl
Tricia Brown, 1995

Mayeros: A Yucatec Maya Family
George Ancona, 1997

Morning on the Lake
Jan Waboose, 1998

Quilted Landscape: Conversations with Young Immigrants
Yale Strom, 1996

Snowflake Bentley
Jacqueline Martin, 1998

Spring Across America
Seymour Simon, 1996

Stars and Planets
David H. Levy, ed., 1996

Under My Nose
Lois Ehlert, 1996

What Color Is Camouflage?
Carolyn Otto, 1996

Winter Across America
Seymour Simon, 1994

A Year on Monhegan Island
Julia Dean, 1994

Writing a Classroom Report

The Amazing Potato: A Story in Which the Incas, Conquistadors, Marie Antoinette, Thomas Jefferson, Wars, Famines, Immigrants, and French Fries All Play a Part
Milton Melzer, 1992

Frozen Man
David Getz, 1994

The Grolier Perfect Report Library, 1992
Volumes 1-3: Vocabulary Improvement Guide
Volume 4: Style Manual
Volume 5: Grammatical Handbook

How Fish Swim
Jill Bailey, 1996

How on Earth Do We Recycle Paper?
Helen Jill Fletcher and Seli Groves, 1993

It Happened in America: True Stories from the Fifty States
Lila Perl, 1993

It Is a Good Day to Die: Indian Eyewitnesses Tell the Story of the Battle of the Little Bighorn
Herman Viola, 1998

The Last Princess: The Story of Princess Ka'iulani of Hawaii
Fay Stanley, 1992

Lights! Camera! Action! How a Movie Is Made
Gail Gibbons, 1985

Lives of the Writers: Comedies, Tragedies (and What the Neighbors Thought)
Kathleen Krull, 1994

A River Ran Wild: An Environmental History
Lynne Cherry, 1993

Rope Burn
Jan Siebold, 1998

Season of the Cranes
Peter Roop, 1989

Surrounded by Sea: Life on a New England Fishing Island
Gail Gibbons, 1991

Talking Walls
Margy Burns Knight, 1992

We the People: The Constitution of the United States of America
Peter Spier, 1987

Weather Forecasting
Gail Gibbons, 1993

Weather Words and What They Mean
Gail Gibbons, 1990

Where on Earth: A Geografunny Guide to the Globe
Paul Rosenthal, 1993

Writing Fantasies

Aliens for Lunch
Jonathan Etra and Stephanie Spinner, 1991

Attic Mice
Ethel Pochocki, 1993

Babe, the Gallant Pig
Dick King-Smith, 1983

Bright Shadow
Avi, 1994

Catwings
Ursula K. LeGuin, 1988

Charlie and the Chocolate Factory
Roald Dahl, 1964

The Computer Nut
Betsy Byars, 1984

The Day of the Unicorn
Mollie Hunter, 1994

Dinosaur Habitat
Helen Griffith, 1998

The Dragon's Boy
Jane Yolen, 1990

Faith and the Rocket Cat
Patrick Jennings, 1998

The Five Sisters
Margaret Mahy, 1997

Flat Stanley
Jeff Brown, 1964

The Garden of Abdul Gasazi
Chris Van Allsburg, 1979

Harriet's Hare
Dick King-Smith, 1995

The Hoboken Chicken Emergency
Daniel M. Pinkwater, 1977

Inside My Feet: The Story of a Giant
Richard Kennedy, 1991

Instead of Three Wishes
Megan Turner, 1995

Into the Land of the Unicorns
Bruce Coville, 1994

The Islander
Cynthia Rylant, 1998

Jacob and the Stranger
Sally Derby, 1994

The King's Equal
Katherine Paterson, 1992

Knights of the Kitchen Table
Jon Scieszka, 1993

The Lion, the Witch, and the Wardrobe
C. S. Lewis, 1950

The Mystery of Pony Hollow
Lynn Hall, 1992

Writing Fantasies
(*continued*)

Nonstop Nonsense
Margaret Mahy, 1977

The Old Banjo
Dennis Haseley, 1983

Poppy
Avi, 1995

Redwall
Brian Jacques, 1986

Roxaboxen
Alice McLerran, 1991

The Same Place but Different
Perry Nodelman, 1995

Songs in the Silence
Catherine Murphy, 1994

A String in the Harp
Nancy Bond, 1976

The 13th Floor
Sid Fleischman, 1995

Undone
Paul Jennings, 1995

The Van Gogh Cafe
Cynthia Rylant, 1995

Writing Tall Tales

American Indian Myths and Legends
Richard Erdoes and Alfonso Ortiz, eds., 1984

American Tall Tales
Mary Pope Osborne, 1991

Big Men, Big Country: A Collection of American Tall Tales
James Bernardin, 1993

Bo Rabbit Smart for True: Tall Tales from the Gullah
Priscilla Jaquith, 1995

Cut from the Same Cloth: American Women of Myth, Legend, and Tall Tale
Robert D. San Souci, 1993

The Elephant's Bathtub: Wonder Tales from the Far East
Frances Carpenter, 1962

Febold Feboldson
Arian Dewey, 1984

Fin M'Coul: The Giant of Knockmany Hill
Tomie dePaola, 1981

How Glooskap Outwits the Ice Giant and the Other Tales of the Maritime Indians
Howard Norman, 1989

The Ink Drinker
Eric Sanvoisin, 1998

Iva Dunnit and the Big Wind
by Carol Purdy, 1985

Jimmy the Pickpocket of the Palace
Donna Jo Napoli, 1995

John Henry
Julius Lester, 1994

John Henry: Steel-Driving Man
C. J. Naden, 1980

Johnny Appleseed
Steven Kellogg, 1992

The Kingdom Under the Sea and Other Stories
Joan Aiken, 1986

Mountain Jack Tales
Gail Haley, 1992

Mr. Yowder and the Train Robbers
Glen Rounds, 1981

Paul Bunyan
Louis Sabin, 1985

Pecos Bill
Steven Kellogg, 1986

Sally Ann Thunder Ann Whirlwind Crockett
Caron Lee Cohen, 1993

Smart Dog
Vivian Vande Velde, 1998

Summer Reading Is Killing Me
Jon Scieszka, 1998

Tell Me a Tale: A Book About Storytelling
Joseph Bruchac, 1997

True Lies: 18 Tales for You to Judge
George Shannon, 1997

Writing Realistic Stories

Afternoon of the Elves
Janet Taylor Lisle, 1989

All the Money in the World
Bill Brittain, 1979

A Blue-Eyed Daisy
Cynthia Rylant, 1985

Box Top Dreams
Miriam Glassman, 1998

The Cat Ate My Gymsuit
Paula Danziger, 1980

The Cay
Theodore Taylor, 1987

The Chalk Box Kid
Clyde Robert Bulla, 1987

The Christmas Cup
Nancy Ruth Patterson, 1989

Felita
Nicholasa Mohr, 1979

The Flimflam Man
Darleen Beard, 1998

Flying Solo
Ralph Fletcher, 1998

Fourth Grade Rats
Jerry Spinelli, 1991

The Gift
Joan Lowery Nixon, 1983

Goodbye My Island
Jean Rogers, 1983

Goodbye, Vietnam
by Gloria Whelan, 1993

Harry's Mad
Dick King-Smith, 1990

The Heart of a Chief
Joseph Bruchac, 1998

Heaven
Angela Johnson, 1998

Hot and Cold Summer
Johanna Hurwitz, 1984

The Hundred Dresses
Eleanor Estes, 1944

It's Like This, Cat
Emily Cheney Neville, 1991

Journey
Patricia MacLachlan, 1991

Julian, Secret Agent
Ann Cameron, 1988

Julian's Glorious Summer
Ann Cameron, 1987

June Bug and the Reverend
Alice Mead, 1998

Kid Power
Susan Pfeffer, 1977

The King of Dragons
Carol Fenner, 1998

King Shoes and Clown Pockets
Faye Gibbons, 1989

Look Back, Moss
Betty Levin, 1998

Me, Mop, and the Moondance Kid
Walter Dean Myers, 1988

Miracle at the Plate
Matt Christopher, 1967

Mississippi Bridge
Mildred D. Taylor, 1990

Mrs. Fish, Ape, and Me, the Dump Queen
Norma Fox Mazer, 1980

My Side of the Mountain
Jean George, 1988

The Not-Just-Anybody Family (and sequels)
Betsy Byars, 1986

Ramona Forever
Beverly Cleary, 1979

Roll of Thunder, Hear My Cry
Mildred D. Taylor, 1976

Secret Letters from 0 to 10
Susie Morgenstern, 1998

The Secret Life of Amanda K. Woods
Ann Cameron, 1998

Shoeshine Girl
Clyde Robert Bulla, 1975

Sister Anne's Hands
Marybeth Lorbiecki, 1998

Soup
Robert Newton Peck, 1974

Starting School with an Enemy
Elisa Carbone, 1998

Stone Fox
John R. Gardiner, 1980

A Summer to Die
Lois Lowry, 1977

Sun & Spoon
Kevin Henkes, 1997

Tales from the Homeplace: Adventures of a Texas Farm Girl
Harriet Burandt, 1997

A Taste of Blackberries
Doris B. Smith, 1973

Thirteen Ways to Sink a Sub
Jamie Gilson, 1982

The Wall
Eve Bunting, 1990

While No One Was Watching
Jane Conly, 1998

The Wild Kid
Harry Mazer, 1998

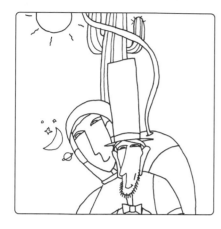

Writing Stories from History

Adventure on the Wilderness Road, 1775
Laurie Lawlor, 1999

Amistad Rising: A Story of Freedom
Veronica Chambers, 1998
[18th-century slavery]

And Then What Happened, Paul Revere?
Jean Fritz, 1973
[American Revolution]

A Band of Angels: A Story Inspired by the Jubilee Singers
Deborah Hopkinson, 1998
[Late 19th-century America]

Bandit's Moon
Sid Fleischman, 1998
[Old West/America]

The Cabin Faced West
Jean Fritz, 1958
[American frontier]

The Courage of Sarah Noble
Alice Dalgliesh, 1954
[18th-century America]

Dawn of Fear
Susan Cooper, 1970
[Horror of war/England]

Double Life of Pocahontas
Jean Fritz, 1983
[Colonial America]

Fire, Bed, and Bone
Henrietta Branford, 1998
[14th-century England]

A Gift for Mama
Esther Hautzig, 1981
[Jewish perspective pre-World War II]

Guests
Michael Dorris, 1994
[Colonial America]

Hannah
Gloria Whelan, 1991
[Late 19th-century America]

I Am an American: A True Story of Japanese Internment
Jerry Stanley, 1994
[World War II]

I Am Regina
Sally M. Keehn, 1991
[French/Indian War]

The Iron Dragon Never Sleeps
Stephen Krensky, 1994
[Post-Civil War/West]

Jar of Dreams
Yoshiko Uchida, 1981
[Depression/America]

Jim Ugly
Sid Fleischman, 1992
[Old West/America]

Katie's Trunk
Ann Turner, 1992
[American Revolution]

Lily's Crossing
Patricia Reilly Giff, 1997
[World War II]

Lion to Guard Us
Clyde Robert Bulla, 1981
[Colonial America]

Little House on the Prairie
Laura Ingalls Wilder, 1953
[American frontier]

Morning Girl
Michael Dorris, 1992
[15th-century America]

My Name Is Not Angelica
Scott O'Dell, 1990
[18th-century slavery]

Number the Stars
Lois Lowry, 1989
[World War II]

Pioneer Cat
William H. Hooks, 1988
[Old West/America]

A Pioneer Sampler: The Daily Life of a Pioneer Family in 1840
Barbara Greenwood, 1994
[Old West/America]

Pocahontas and the Strangers
Clyde Robert Bulla, 1971
[Colonial America]

The Printer's Apprentice
Stephen Krensky, 1995
[Colonial America]

Sadako and the Thousand Paper Cranes
Eleanor Coerr, 1977
[Nuclear war]

Sarah, Plain and Tall
Patricia MacLachlan, 1985
[American frontier]

The Secret Soldier: The Story of Deborah Sampson
Ann McGovern, 1975
[American Revolution]

Soft Rain: A Story of the Cherokee Trail of Tears
Cornelia Cornelissen, 1998
[Old West/America]

Somewhere Around the Corner
Jackie French, 1995
[1930's Australia]

Surprising Myself
Jean Fritz, 1992
[Researching historical biographies]

A Titanic Journey Across the Sea, 1912
Laurie Lawlor, 1998

Trouble River
Betsy Byars, 1969
[American frontier]

V Is for Victory: America Remembers World War II
Kathleen Krull, 1995

Voyage to a Free Land, 1630
Laurie Lawlor, 1999
[Colonial America]

West Along the Wagon Road, 1852
Laurie Lawlor, 1998

When Hitler Stole Pink Rabbit
Judith Kerr, 1971
[World War II]

Writing Plays

Aesop's Fables: Plays for Young Children
Dr. Albert Cullum, 1993

Frantic Frogs and Other Frankly Fractured Folktales for Readers Theatre
Anthony Fredericks, 1993

Plays: The Drama Magazine for Young People
Published by Plays, Inc.

Scary Readers Theatre
Suzanne L. Barchers, 1994

Writing Poems

And the Green Grass Grew All Around: Folk Poetry for Everyone
Collected by Alvin Schwartz, 1992

The Book of Pigericks
Arnold Lobel, 1983

Celebration: The Story of American Holidays
Lucille Recht Penner, 1993

Creatures of Earth, Sea, and Sky
Georgia Heard, 1992

Dinosaur Dances
Jane Yolen, 1990

Dogs and Dragons, Trees and Dreams
Karla Kuskin, 1980

Eats Poems
Arnold Adoff, 1979

Hey World, Here I Am!
Jean Little, 1989

Honey, I Love and Other Love Poems
Eloise Greenfield, 1978

How to Write Poetry
Paul Janeczko, 1999

I Am Writing a Poem About . . . a Game of Poetry
Myra Cohn Livingston, ed., 1997

Joyful Noise: Poems for Two Voices
Paul Fleischman, 1988

Lives: Poems About Famous Americans
Lee Bennett Hopkins, ed., 1999

Marty Frye, Private Eye
Janet Tashjian, 1998

Marvelous Math: A Book of Poems
Lee Bennett Hopkins, ed., 1997

The Mouse of Amherst
Elizabeth Spires, 1999

My Song Is Beautiful: Poems and Pictures in Many Voices
Selected by Mary Ann Hoberman, 1994

Rainbow Writing
Eve Merriam, 1976

The Random House Book of Poetry for Children
Jack Prelutsky, ed., 1983

Sir Galahad, Mr. Longfellow, and Me
Betty Horvath, 1998

Street Rhymes Around the World
Jane Yolen, 1992

The Trees Stand Shining: Poetry of the North American Indians
Collected by Hettie Jones, 1993

Very Best (Almost) Friends: Poems of Friendship
Paul Janeczko, 1999

Wind in the Long Grass: A Collection of Haiku
William J. Higginson, ed., 1992

The Writing Bug
Lee Bennett Hopkins, 1993

Writing Riddles

Behind the King's Kitchen: A Roster of Rhyming Riddles
William Jay Smith, 1992

Eight Ate: A Feast of Homonym Riddles
Marvin Terban, 1982

Funny You Should Ask: How to Make Up Jokes and Riddles with Wordplay
Marvin Terban, 1992

Geographunny
Mort Gerberg, 1991

Hey, Hay! A Wagonful of Funny Homonym Riddles
Marvin Terban, 1990

How Do You Get a Horse Out of a Bathtub?
Louis Phillips, 1983

Ji-Nongo-Nongo Means Riddles
Verna Aardema, 1978

Lightning Inside You and Other Native American Riddles
John Biehorst, ed., 1992

Petcetera: The Pet Riddle Book
Meyer Seltzer, 1988

Puppy Riddles
Katy Hall, 1998

Riddle Roundup
Giulio Maestro, 1989

Riddles to Tell Your Cat
Caroline Levine, 1992

Ridiculous Nicholas Pet Riddles
Joseph Rosenbloom, 1981

Unriddling: All Sorts of Riddles to Puzzle Your Guessery
Alvin Schwartz, ed., 1983

Westward Ho Ho Ho! Jokes from the Wild West
Victoria Hartman, 1993

What's a Frank Frank? Tasty Homograph Riddles
Giulio Maestro, 1984

With One White Wing: Puzzles in Poems and Pictures
Elizabeth Spires, 1995

Using the Library

Aunt Chip and the Great Triple Creek Dam Affair
Patricia Polacco, 1996

The Library Card
Jerry Spinelli, 1997

Library Lil
Suzanne Williams, 1997

Richard Wright and the Library Card
William Miller, 1997

Tomas and the Library Lady
Pata Mora, 1997

Computers and Internet Use

E-Mail
Larry Dane Brimner, 1997

50 Fun Ways to Internet: How to Sign On, Navigate, and Explore the Net Without Getting Lost in Cyberspace
Allan Hoffman, 1998

A Guide to the World Wide Web
Lory Hawkes, 1998

Mousetracks: A Kid's Computer Idea Book
Peggy L. Steinhauser, 1997

The World Wide Web
Charnan Kazunas and Tom Kazunas, 1997

The Historical Time Line

Dateline: Troy
Paul Fleischman, 1996

The DK Visual Time Line of the 20th Century
Simon Adams, 1996

Dorling Kindersley Visual Time Line of Transportation
Anthony Wilson, 1995

Smithsonian Visual Time Line of Inventions
Richard Platt, 1994

Time Lines: Entertainment
Jacqueline Morley, 1994

Time Lines: Flight
David Jefferis, 1994

Time Lines: Food
Richard Tames, 1994

Time Lines: Inventions
Peter Turvey, 1994

Reading-Homework Contract

I am expected to read at home for at least [ ] minutes.

I understand that I may choose the books and also the times and the days that I will read. I also understand that during this reading-homework time, I am to read well-selected material. (Certain magazines, comic books, catalogs, and picture books are not acceptable.)

[ ] I did read and understand the above information. I can keep track of my own reading homework and will report it on the reverse side of this sheet.

[ ] I did read and understand the above information. I will have someone at home help me keep track of and report my reading homework.

_____   _____
(Student signature)   (Teacher signature)

_____   _____
(Date)   (Date)

_____   _____
(Parent signature)   (Date)

Books I Have Read

BOOK TITLE	Number of Pages	Author	I give this book ★/☆☆/★★/★★★/☆☆☆☆

Thinking and Learning Strategies

The thinking and learning strategies on the following pages cover important areas often included in a complete language program.

Writing to Learn

What is "writing to learn"?

Writing to learn is a method of learning that students can use in all subjects at all ages. It is thinking on paper—thinking to discover connections, describe processes, express newly discovered ideas, raise questions, and find answers.

How can I get started with writing to learn?

Before incorporating writing-to-learn activities into your curriculum, remember these key points:

■ The main purpose of writing-to-learn activities is to promote better thinking and learning; better writing is a by-product.

■ Since writing-to-learn activities allow students to personalize learning, they understand better and remember longer.

■ Writing to learn is not a "program." Writing-to-learn activities complement the curriculum already being used in different subject areas.

How do I implement writing-to-learn?

■ With your students, turn to pages 353-355 in *Writers Express* to develop an understanding of writing to learn.

■ Select writing-to-learn activities that suit your subject area and allow your students to become more independent and more actively involved in the learning process.

■ Help students understand that they are "writing to learn" and not "writing to show learning." With writing-to-learn activities, they are not writing to please you, the teacher, but to personalize and better understand information.

What other strategies can I use to incorporate writing-to-learn activities?

• Use any of the writing-to-learn activities listed on pages 172-173.
• Use journal writing regularly in your classroom to develop students' responding and thinking skills.

Class Journal ● You may have students use a notebook journal to respond to class-related work and events. For example, after you introduce a new concept in science, have students predict what might happen next. Or ask students to respond to a class discussion or a film. Class journals work especially well for responding to reading (whether a chapter in a science text or a novel). Class discussions become more engaging when students have first responded in their journals and then are able to articulate those responses. Class journals can help students raise questions, develop answers, and respond to any class activity.

Project Journal ● This journal is like the class journal except that it is a more independent writing-to-learn tool. Students use this journal to keep track of their progress on a project over a period of days or weeks. They may raise questions, document their successes, or evaluate their group or individual effectiveness on a particular project. Project journals, like class journals, allow students to jot down new vocabulary related to the class or project, record important or confusing ideas, make predictions about what might happen, and connect concepts to personal experiences and ideas.

Personal Journal ● This notebook allows the student to respond independently. Responses and reflections are not assigned. The student uses this notebook (sometimes called a learning log) to question, describe, and articulate concepts discovered in various classes. Such writing allows students to develop abstract thinking skills. They may choose to use this journal as a communication tool to dialogue with the teacher about questions or concerns.

Collaborative Learning

We have all participated in collaborative groups at some point in our lives—in our families, with friends, in sports activities. Cooperation is an essential skill for functioning successfully in society. Collaborative learning means "working together." It differs from group work in that collaborative learning stresses positive interdependence among students, face-to-face interaction, individual accountability, interpersonal and small-group skills, and group processing. These basic elements can lead students to high achievement, positive attitudes toward subject areas, and stronger critical-thinking skills.

How can I get started with collaborative learning?

As you begin implementing collaborative groups in your classroom, remember these key points:

- Collaborative learning can be used successfully with any type of academic activity, but it works best with activities that involve problem solving, decision making, or creative thinking.

- Collaborative groups should be relatively small (2-6 students) and should contain students of varied abilities.

- Students must learn and practice collaborative skills before cooperative learning can be successful.

- With collaborative learning, the teacher's role changes from lecturer to classroom manager. The teacher structures learning groups, teaches basic concepts and strategies, then monitors group functioning and intervenes when necessary.

How do I implement collaborative learning?

There are a number of issues to consider:

- Begin by teaching students collaborative skills. Review pages 330-331 and 360-365 of *Writers Express* for ideas about developing listening skills and group skills.

- Decide on the size of student groups and a room arrangement (desks or tables arranged in small groups) to best implement collaborative learning.

- Design learning tasks that will be best accomplished through collaborative learning. (Don't assign a task to the group that can best be completed individually.)

- Introduce concepts and strategies to the whole class.

- Divide students into assigned groups and provide them with roles (such as reader, recorder, encourager) to fill within the group.

- Monitor group functioning and intervene when clarification of tasks or roles is necessary.

- After the task is completed, review the process. Discuss successes and areas that require better group functioning.

Strategies for Implementing Collaborative Learning

Experiment with some of these collaborative activities before deciding if this classroom strategy works for you and your students. These activities can be applied in any subject area.

Preparing for a Test

Recommended Group and Size:
A heterogeneous group of four students

Group Skills to Emphasize:
"Skills for Listening" (page 362)
"Skills for Clarifying" (page 363)

Other Skills to Emphasize:
"Taking Good Notes" (pages 374-375)

The Process:
Step 1: One student reads a question and explains step-by-step how to answer it correctly.

Step 2: The other group members check for accuracy. For any question that is disputed, the group must find the page number and paragraph where the correct answer is located.

Step 3: Rotating clockwise, the next students reads the next question and repeats the process.

Assessment:
Each student in the group takes the test individually. If *all* group members exceed their scores from a previous test, each will receive five bonus points.

Making Classroom Presentations

Recommended Group and Size:
A heterogeneous group of four students

Group Skills to Emphasize:
"Skills for Listening" (page 362)
"Skills for Cooperating" (page 363)
"Skills for Clarifying" (page 363)

Other Skills to Emphasize:
"Giving Speeches" (pages 311-317)
"Multimedia Computer Reports"
(pages 204-207)

The Process:
Step 1: Students work together in their groups to prepare a presentation on an assigned topic. Students create visual aids and rehearse presentations. Each student practices the group's presentation so that he or she can individually present to other groups.

Step 2: The class is divided into four groups and placed at different locations in the room. Each group member makes the group's presentation individually to one of the four classroom groups.

Assessment:
Each student must make a presentation to a small group from the class.

Taking Accurate Notes

Recommended Group Size:
Two students

Group Skills to Emphasize:
"Skills for Listening" (page 362)
"Skills for Clarifying" (page 363)

Other Skills to Emphasize:
"Taking Good Notes" (pages 374-375)

The Process:
Step 1: After a lesson, one student orally summarizes his or her notes for the partner student.

Step 2: This other student discusses the information presented, perhaps asking for clarification or correcting certain facts.

Step 3: Both students improve their notes by making corrections and adding information from their partner's work.

Assessment:
The teacher randomly selects the notes of one group member to evaluate for completeness and accuracy.

Learning to Think

Of course your students are already thinking! They are recalling, observing, comparing, analyzing, and evaluating information all the time. Encouraging clear, creative thinking is the goal of any effective learning environment. Here are some ways to make your classroom more "thinking oriented."

How can I start promoting better thinking skills?

As you consider ways to develop and promote thinking skills in your classroom, remember these key points:

- Creative learning activities and environments enhance thinking skills.
- Students' thinking skills will improve through modeling, practice, and experimentation.

How can I implement better thinking skills?

- Personalize the learning in your classroom. Students will approach learning more thoughtfully when the subject matter means something to them personally.
- Promote creative activities that enhance thinking skills: writing stories, poems, riddles, songs; doing problem solving; working on inventions.
- Encourage collaborative learning. Collaborative learning provides students with one of the most powerful ways to learn and think—through verbalization.
- Challenge students to think and act for themselves by asking open-ended questions and by initiating role-playing activities, dramatic scenarios, and discussions. Give students opportunities to explore, take risks, and make mistakes.
- Discuss different kinds of thinking and ways to think clearly. (See the thinking section in *Writers Express*, pages 338-351, for help.)
- Help students think about their own learning and connect what they have already learned to new information.

Strategies for Developing and Promoting Thinking Skills

Using pages 338-344 of *Writers Express*, explore different types of thinking with your students. Use the following terms as you focus on thinking across the curriculum and throughout the year.

Recalling

- Use listing, freewriting, or clustering to recall concepts or ideas discussed in any subject area. (See *Writers Express*, page 36.)
- Have students create a dictionary that defines the important terms discussed in a unit.

Understanding

- After discussing a new idea or concept, have students write a paragraph that explains what they've learned about that concept. Then ask them to share the paragraph with a classmate and compare their work, adding information as necessary.
- Ask students to demonstrate their understanding of a concept by preparing a brief oral explanation. Encourage creativity by asking them to present their explanations in unique ways—doing a rap, presenting a play, or using visual aids.

Applying

- After students learn how to count money, have them write story problems that demonstrate their ability to apply this concept in real life.
- After a unit on the environment, have students explore ways to reduce, reuse, and recycle at home and in school.

Analyzing

- After studying plants in science class, have students draw and label diagrams that illustrate the life cycle of a bean plant.
- After a social studies unit about early American life, have students write a paragraph contrasting life in early America to life today.

Synthesizing

- After a social studies unit about early explorers, have students write a play, placing themselves in the roles of the explorers and the people on their expeditions.
- After students have read a chapter from a novel, ask them to predict what might happen next and share their predictions with their classmates.

Evaluating

- After discussing a topic as a class, divide students into collaborative groups and have them explore the good and bad points of that topic. Then have them write a paragraph expressing their opinion.
- After working in collaborative groups, have students evaluate how successfully the groups met their goals.

Thinking in Action

Practice these problem-solving, decision-making, and clear-thinking strategies with your students. Return to the handbook throughout the school year as situations in class work and school life call for the following thinking strategies.

Problem-Solving Strategies

- After a lesson or presentation about an environmental problem, have students in small groups follow the steps listed on page 351 in *Writers Express* to discover possible solutions.
- Read aloud a chapter from a novel in which the main character faces a problem. Stop reading before the problem is resolved and ask students to write in their journals about how they would continue the story and have the character solve the problem.

Decision-Making Strategies

- Have students participate in decisions that affect your classroom. Perhaps they can help decide on the location for a class field trip. Present to the students two or three trip options; then arrange them in small groups to work through the decision—using the guidelines listed on page 350 in *Writers Express*. Have groups share their results with the class.

Clear-Thinking Strategies

- Read your students a short essay that contains a combination of factual statements and opinion statements. Discuss which statements are factual and which are opinions. (*Writers Express* page 347 will help.)
- Examine some TV, magazine, and newspaper advertisements with your students. Distinguish between the facts and the opinions presented in the advertisements. (See *Writers Express* page 328 for more information about viewing commercials.)

Building Vocabulary

We know there is a strong connection between a student's vocabulary and his or her listening, speaking, and writing ability. The stronger a student's vocabulary, the more effectively he or she is able to communicate. The following section provides insights and strategies for helping students build their vocabulary skills.

How can I get started?

Before beginning to implement strategies for improving vocabulary, remember these key points:

- Vocabulary development must occur across the curriculum. Students must read, hear, speak, and write the words they are attempting to learn in all of their classes.
- Giving students lists of vocabulary words with little or no context is not an efficient way to teach vocabulary.
- Students learn words by connecting them to their own experiences.

How can students begin building their vocabulary skills?

- Examine and discuss with your students the vocabulary section in *Writers Express* (pages 288-305).
- Involve students in creating vocabulary lists. Choose from relevant themes, topics, subjects, and events in the classroom.
- Encourage students to collect personal vocabulary words in their journals. Help them analyze each personal and classroom vocabulary word using a dictionary, glossary, or thesaurus.
- Teach students how to use context to determine meanings of new vocabulary words. (*Writers Express* page 289 can help.)
- Design writing activities that encourage students to use newly acquired vocabulary words in context.

Strategies for Building Vocabulary Skills

In addition to the strategies provided in *Writers Express* (pages 288-305), try the following vocabulary-building activities:

- Select five or six words from a chapter or selection students are about to read. Direct them to the locations of the words in the text, and ask them to write down what they think each word means. Discuss possible meanings and arrive at correct definitions from context.
- Select a word from one of your class vocabulary lists. Show students how to use a thesaurus to find a word and its synonyms. Have partners each select a word from the vocabulary list, look it up in a thesaurus, and share its synonyms with their partners.
- Play a dictionary game, choosing a word from the class list. Without saying the word, tell students the word's definition. Have students race to find the correct word in their dictionaries. The student who finds the correct word first chooses the next definition.
- Encourage students (in small groups or individually) to make up their own word games. These promote creative exploration of new vocabulary words.
- Have students create their own dictionaries of words and definitions that relate to specific themes (such as computers, music, or favorite sports).
- At the beginning of each day, print a new vocabulary word on the board. As students enter the room, they immediately grab a dictionary and look up the word. As a class, students discuss the word and agree on its definition. They then use the word correctly in a sentence, showing that they know what the word means. A written quiz can be given each Friday, covering the five words from the past week.

Improving Student Spelling

Students learn to spell over time through experiences with words. Because spelling is a special cognitive process connected to writing and reading, teach it in context—not isolation. Teaching in context helps students see that correct spelling allows writers—themselves included—to communicate ideas clearly. The following section will help you design an effective spelling program.

Getting Started

Before implementing a variety of spelling activities, remember these key points:

- Spelling ability is not an indicator of intelligence. Students who have difficulty with spelling tend to process information holistically while good spellers tend to process information sequentially.
- Effective spelling programs encourage students to explore relationships between letters and sounds and to discover word patterns. Active word play is a helpful learning tool.
- Spelling improves when students understand why words are spelled the way they are.

Note: Memorizing word lists does not transfer to daily writing.

Guidelines for Teaching Spelling

- Involve students in developing a class spelling list of frequently used words and words from topics explored in class. Study these words in fairly short lists.
- From the class list, help students develop personal spelling lists that fit their abilities, interests, and needs.
- Follow a pretest-study-test pattern. Have students correct their own pretests.
- Focus on sounds and structures of words so that students begin to recognize patterns and develop generalizations.
- Conduct ongoing analysis of spelling errors so that students learn to self-correct their spelling.

- Teach spelling through the many activities students participate in each day.
- Associate spelling words with students' previous knowledge.
- Write often and build proofreading activities into the writing process.

Strategies for Improving Student Spelling

Consider the following activities and ideas when planning weekly spelling units.

Minilessons: Use the spelling-related minilessons in this guide, or create your own.

Pretest: Select 20-25 words from the master list in the handbook (pages 398-401) to use as a pretest at the beginning of the year. Students who have mastered these words should choose words from their personal lists for weekly spelling practice.

Regular Writing: Encourage students to use words from their weekly spelling lists in journal writing, writing assignments, and other writing activities.

Word Searches: Ask students to look for words from their weekly spelling lists in books, magazines, and newspapers as they read in class and on their own.

Mnemonic Devices: Teach students to create and use mnemonics to remember spelling patterns. Share these devices with the class on student-designed posters.

Theme Dictionaries: Have students list and spell correctly key words related to topics studied in all their classes.

Creative Words: Have students use familiar prefixes and suffixes to create new words that could be added to personal spelling lists and used as weekly spelling practice.

Spelling Starts: Use the first 10 minutes of the day to direct spelling instruction. Then apply that instruction throughout the day's reading and writing activities.

Weekly Spelling Words for Grade 4

1 (Days and holidays)
Friday
Labor Day
Monday
Saturday
Sunday
Thursday
Tuesday
Wednesday

2 (Double consonants)
called
full
guess
lesson
little
office
pretty
tomorrow

3 (Math words)
arithmetic
divide
fifty
forty
fourth
half
none
second

4 (-ing endings)
beginning
building
coming
getting
having
making
studying
writing

5 (Months)
April
August
December
February
January
July
November
October

6 (Months and holidays)
Fourth of July
June
March
May
New Year's Day
September
Thanksgiving
Veterans Day

7 (-y endings)
buy
day
emergency
every
family
holiday
many
party

8 (Prepositions)
about
above
across
against
outside
through
until
upon

9 (Adjectives)
busy
careful
easy
juicy
important
loose
nice
tired

10 (Long $\bar{a}$ sound)
afraid
angel
face
famous
place
played
safety
table

11 (Consonant blends and digraphs)
grocery
practice
present
problem
sandwich
straight
trouble
which

12 (Compound words)
birthday
breakfast
careless
classroom
everybody
football
handkerchief
sometimes

13 (Consonant blends and digraphs)
choose
principal
skillful
strike
there
what
when
where

14 (Consonant blends and digraphs)
athlete
buckle
climate
closet
history
school
started
young

15 (Prepositions)
after
among
around
before
behind
between
since
within

16 Semester Review

Weekly Spelling Words for Grade 4

17 (Contractions)
couldn't
haven't
he's
it'll
she'd
shouldn't
they're
we're

18 (Plurals)
children
classmates
eyes
hundreds
people
shoes
toys
women

19 (Silent letters)
answer
climb
doubt
island
listen
whole
write
wrote

20 (Spelled with *ie*)
achieve
believe
chief
fierce
friend
piece
quiet
thief

21 (*o* sounds like *ŭ*)
come
does
done
from
front
money
nothing
other

22 (Spelled with *or* or *ur*)
century
church
morning
pasture
shore
store
surprise
turn

23 (One-syllable words)
cough
edge
gone
quit
rough
scene
use
were

24 (Consonant blends and digraphs)
belong
blanket
brought
bruise
distance
instead
scared
while

25 (-*er* endings)
brother
customer
letter
neither
number
quarter
together
weather

26 (-*or* endings)
author
color
doctor
flavor
honor
mayor
senior
visitor

27 (Spelled with *ea*)
already
earth
peace
pleasant
please
pleasure
teacher
tear

28 (Spelled with *oi* or *ai*)
choir
entertain
explain
noisy
point
poison
said
voice

29 (Three-syllable words)
apartment
avenue
bicycle
calendar
discover
exercise
natural
vacation

30 (Adverbs)
early
later
never
once
quickly
soon
very
yesterday

31 (Spelled with *ou*)
counting
courage
court
cousin
enough
found
hour
should

32 Semester Review

Weekly Spelling Words for Grade 5

1 (Food words)
banana
biscuit
cafeteria
casserole
dessert
salad
sugar
vegetable

2 (Spelled with *ea*)
beautiful
great
heard
heavy
league
nuclear
reason
reveal

3 (Contractions)
aren't
he'd
I'm
she'll
they've
wouldn't
you'll
you're

4 (Nouns)
avenue
courage
feel
hospital
knives
magazine
quotient
vehicle

5 (Double consonants)
community
difficulty
grammar
impossible
mirror
opposite
parallel
suppose

6 (Silent letters)
built
business
campaign
foreign
gadget
knife
knowledge
whose

7 (Consonant blends and digraphs)
accept
athletic
chimney
chocolate
elephant
fragile
length
products

8 (People words)
burglar
candidate
character
genius
guard
immigrant
individual
musician

9 (Spelled with *ei*)
eight
either
height
leisure
neither
receive
weight
weird

10 (-e endings)
advise
allowance
article
baggage
bruise
done
prejudice
trouble

11 (Spelled with *ai*)
afraid
bargain
captain
certain
dairy
entertain
raise
straight

12 (Long *a* sound)
ache
ancient
canine
gymnasium
occasion
operate
patience
safety

13 (Two-syllable words)
angle
blizzard
canyon
fashion
music
obey
system
volume

14 (Adjectives)
accurate
ancient
brilliant
expensive
grateful
handsome
several
terrible

15 (Adjectives)
actual
awful
curious
different
familiar
favorite
gentle
noisy

16 Semester Review

Weekly Spelling Words for Grade 5

17 (Verbs)
appreciate
complete
developed
forward
manufacture
package
recognize
thought

21 (-ous endings)
anonymous
dangerous
delicious
disastrous
enormous
generous
hazardous
humorous

25 (Four-syllable words)
celebration
congratulate
definition
environment
experience
fortunately
graduation
psychology

29 (Words with suffixes)
attractive
discussion
expression
government
guardian
happened
interested
traveling

18 (Words with prefixes)
absent
adventure
disappear
division
impatient
paragraph
unconscious
unusual

22 (Double consonants)
accident
application
arrival
caterpillar
happiness
horrible
millions
swimming

26 (Spelled with ou)
amount
courteous
encourage
fountain
journal
mountain
route
surround

30 (Spelled with au)
audience
automobile
autumn
exhausted
faucet
gauge
laughed
restaurant

19 (Consonant blends and digraphs)
although
awhile
bought
describe
language
privilege
though
thousands

23 (Adverbs)
exactly
finally
generally
immediately
quite
suddenly
unfortunately
usually

27 (Four-syllable words)
accompany
advertisement
artificial
intelligent
literature
mathematics
preparation
temperature

31 (Words with suffixes)
apologize
argument
judgment
lovable
marriage
mysterious
responsibilities
truly

20 (c sounds like s)
cemetery
certificate
civilization
criticize
fierce
icicle
innocent
violence

24 (Double vowels)
agreement
choose
cocoon
committee
cooperate
neighborhood
skiing
vacuum

28 (-y endings)
anniversary
company
courtesy
electricity
geography
jewelry
journey
salary

32 Semester Review

Additional Spelling Activities

Teachers should consider the ideas and activities listed on this page when planning weekly spelling units.

High-Frequency Words ● Words from one of the many published high-frequency lists (words student writers use again and again) could be incorporated into the weekly spelling lists or perhaps into midweek spelling mini-lessons. (Teachers might create sentences containing these high-frequency words for brief dictation sessions.)

Commonly Mixed Pairs ● Teachers should also refer to the using-the-right-word list in the handbook (402-411) for additional words to incorporate into the weekly spelling lists or into midweek spelling minilessons. (Some of these words already appear in the spelling lists.)

Workshops and Minilessons ● Teachers should check the student SkillsBooks for workshops and minilessons related to spelling. These activities could be implemented as spelling practice activities.

Proofreading Practice ● As students practice spelling words for the test, they should be encouraged to employ a basic spelling strategy (examine, pronounce, cover, and write) and repeat this process three or four times to ensure mastery.

Regular Writing ● Ask students to circle from three to five words that they think they have misspelled in their writing. Have them check and correct these words before preparing their writing for publication. (Have students keep track of words they continue to misspell in personal spelling dictionaries.)

Special Note: Make sure students understand that spelling is part of writing, and not an end in itself. Students also need to know that spelling comes into play primarily when they are preparing to go public with their work, and not before.

Writing Activities ● Encourage (or require) students to use words from their weekly spelling lists in journal writing, in regular writing assignments, and in other writing-related activities.

Prefix and Suffix Work ● Students could be provided with a limited number of prefixes and suffixes, and then asked to create as many new words as possible by adding these affixes to selected words in the weekly spelling lists.

Board Work ● Teachers could display two or three of the most challenging words from the spelling list on the board during a class period. Announce that the words will be erased at the end of the period, and the students will be expected to spell them on a slip of paper before dismissal.

Word Searches ● Students could be asked to look for words from their weekly spelling lists in the books, periodicals, and newspapers that they read before, during, and after class.

Specialized Spelling ● Students could be asked to list (and spell correctly) words related to special areas of interest like baseball, astronomy, fashions, and so on. (Students could create their own specialized dictionaries.)

Quarterly Assessment ● Teachers might want to select words from the weekly spelling lists for an end-of-the-quarter assessment test. (Words that are misspelled by many of the students should be worked with again during the next quarter.)

Minilessons

The following pages contain more than 150 minilessons that you and your students can use with the *Writers Express* handbook. These minilessons cover the important skills, strategies, and topics addressed in the handbook.

Minilessons
The Process of Writing

A Writer's Question .... A Basic Writing Guide (4-5)

■ **THINK** of a question you have about writing.
  TURN to pages 4-8 of *Writers Express* to see if you can find an answer
  there. If not, **TURN** to the table of contents or the index in your
  handbook, and try to find an answer that way.
  SHARE your results with the class.

Getting Started .... Steps in the Writing Process (4)

■ **WRITE** about your personal "process" of writing.
  ASK yourself: How do I decide on a topic? What do I do next?
  COMPARE your process to the one described on handbook pages 8 and 9.
  Using pages 10 and 11, **LIST** an idea or two that you plan to try for
  each of the four main steps in the writing process.

Why Five? .... Steps in the Writing Process (5)

■ **MAKE** a poster with the title "Why Five Steps?"
  LIST the five steps of the writing process. After each step, **WRITE** one
  sentence telling why it is important.
  USE different colors, drawings, and so on, to make your poster interesting
  and fun to read.

Focus Pocus .... One Writer's Process (4)

■ **GET** four index cards. On the first card, **LIST** words that come to mind
  when you think about a favorite teacher. On the second card, **WRITE** a
  sentence that contains one main idea about this teacher. On the third card,
  REWRITE your sentence to make it better, using details that show.
    RECOPY your sentence in your best handwriting on the fourth card,
    making sure every word is correct.

Be a writing detective. . . . . One Writer's Process (5)

- **READ** the character sketch "My Neighbor Betty" on handbook page 154.
  WRITE a paragraph explaining the process the writer followed. Tell how you think the writer chose Betty as her subject, how she gathered details, and so on. Make an educated guess based on what you know about the writing process and what you see in the finished sketch.

Very Effective! . . . . Traits of Effective Writing (4)

- **READ** "Musky Mike's Big Catch" on handbook page 217.
  CHOOSE two traits of effective writing that you see in this story.
  On a sheet of paper, **LIST** the two traits. Under each trait, copy two sentences from the story that are examples of it.

Even Better . . . . Traits of Effective Writing (5)

- **CHOOSE** a piece of your writing.
  IDENTIFY one trait of effective writing that you see in your writing.
  UNDERLINE the parts of your writing that show that trait.
  Now **IDENTIFY** one trait of effective writing that is weak or missing.
  REVISE your writing to strengthen that trait.

All Dressed Up . . . . Writing with Computers (4-5)

- **GET** a piece of your writing. If it is not already on your computer, type it in.
  REVISE the computer file of your writing using the guidelines in "Designing Your Writing" on handbook page 26.

A Few Favorites . . . . Planning Your Portfolio (4-5)

- **LIST** some of your favorite pieces of writing that you have done in the past.
  WRITE a sentence or two about each, explaining why they are your favorites.

Life Map .... Choosing a Subject (4)

■ **DRAW** your life map.   Start with your birth and work up to the present.
   CHOOSE the experiences you want to picture along the way.
   SAVE your map in your writing folder to use later for personal writing
      topics.   (See handbook page 37 for a model of a life map.)

Dust off your cluster, buster. .... Choosing a Subject (5)

■ **MAKE** a cluster for a school-related event.
   USE the model on handbook page 36 to get started.
   SAVE it in your writing folder for a future writing topic.

The Shape of Things to Come .... Finding a Form (4-5)

■ **CHOOSE** one of the shorter forms of writing on handbook pages 41-43.
   EXPERIMENT with one of them.   Then **EXCHANGE** your writing with a
      classmate and **RESPOND** to one another's work.

Pencil Talk ...... Gathering Details and Making a Plan (4)

■ **MAKE UP** a dialogue between two pencils who are talking about all the
   writing they have to do in your class.
   KEEP the conversation going as long as you can.
   SAVE your imaginary conversation in your writing folder for future use.

Converse .... Gathering Details and Making a Plan (5)

■ **TURN** to handbook page 46 and read "Talk to Others."   Then **FIND** a partner
   and **TALK** about your writing topic.
   TAKE notes on any ideas your partner suggests for your topic.
   On your own, use your partner's suggestions to develop a writing plan
      following the guidelines on page 47.

Sentence Factory . . . . Writing a First Draft (4)

- ■ **THINK** of an interesting, exciting, or fun experience you have had.
  LIST at least five details about the experience.
  CREATE a first draft by writing a sentence about each detail you listed.
  Put your sentences in the same order as your list, with one exception:
  If you think of an added detail as you are writing, write a sentence
  about it as soon as you think of it. Keep writing until you have a
  sentence for each detail you listed.

Tell me more. Writing a First Draft (5)

- ■ **READ** the first draft of a "middle part" on handbook page 52, and notice the
  list of words above it.
  IMAGINE that you are the writer, and you rode in the underwater craft.
  WRITE two or more sentences to add to the first draft. **USE** two of the
  following ways to do this: *define, argue, compare, contrast.* For
  example, you could *define* a word the writer used, or *compare* this
  experience to going on a nature hike.

Before and After . . . . Revising Your Writing (4-5)

- ■ **WRITE** a short paragraph about a personal experience. Then decide where
  you could add "showing" details to the paragraph, using handbook page 58.
  REWRITE your paragraph with your changes. Which one do you like
  better, the "before" or the "after" paragraph?

Saying the Right Thing . . . . . Revising with Partners (4-5)

- ■ **BRAINSTORM** for 5 minutes about all the ways you can help writing
  partners improve their writing.
  ORGANIZE your ideas on paper, using handbook page 61 for helpful tips.
  FILE the list in your writing folder.
  USE your ideas the next time you conference with a partner.

Check! . . . . Editing and Proofreading (4-5)

■ **FIND** a piece of your writing that needs some editing and proofreading.
   USE the "Editing and Proofreading Checklist" on handbook page 67 as a guide.
   MAKE your corrections, and **WRITE** your final copy if there's time.

It's personal. . . . . Publishing Your Writing (4-5)

■ **USE** the instructions on handbook page 73 to help you make a personal writing book (blank book).
   DESIGN the cover.
   DECIDE whether to use the writing book in school or at home, and **SET** a regular time to write in your book.

Twins . . . . Writing Paragraphs (4)

■ **READ** about "a favorite tree" on handbook pages 78-81.
   THINK of your favorite place to visit.
   CHOOSE one of the models as a guide, and **WRITE** your own paragraph about your favorite place.

Details, Details . . . . Writing Paragraphs (5)

■ **IMAGINE** that you are going to write four paragraphs, all on the same topic: your neighborhood's clean-up day, when you and your neighbors cleaned up trash and made repairs.
   On a sheet of paper, **COMPLETE** the following sentences to tell what kinds of details each of your paragraphs might include:
   1. My descriptive paragraph might include . . .
   2. My narrative paragraph might include . . .
   3. My expository paragraph might include . . .
   4. My persuasive paragraph might include . . .

Read all about it. . . . . Writing Expository Essays (4)

■ With a partner, **THINK** of and write down three good topics for expository essays. One of your topics should be for a comparison and contrast essay. To help you come up with ideas, **TALK** about subjects you are studying and topics you would like to learn about.

What's the big idea? .... Writing Expository Essays (5)

■ **THINK** of and write down three good topics for expository essays that would interest your classmates.

For each topic, **WRITE** a sentence or two explaining why it is a good topic for this kind of essay and for this audience.

We need a night off! ...... Writing Persuasive Essays (4)

■ Below are the titles of three expository essays. For each one, **WRITE** a title for a *persuasive* essay on the same topic. Use your own paper.

Homework: Most Fourth Graders Study Every Night
Lights Out: Fourth Graders Go to Bed Early
School Lunches: Plenty of Peas and Carrots for Fourth Graders

Very Funny .... Writing Persuasive Essays (5)

■ Below are titles for three persuasive essays. **CHOOSE** one of the titles and **COPY** it on a sheet of paper.

Under the title, **WRITE** three (or more) facts, reasons, or details to support the opinion expressed in the title. Use your sense of humor, but be persuasive, too!

Fifth Graders Should Get Extra Credit for Being Great at Computer Games
Fifth Graders Should Create the Menus for School Lunches
Fifth Graders Should Get Out of School Early Every Friday

White Whiskers Twitch .... Descriptive Writing (4)

■ Work with a partner to **DESCRIBE** something in your classroom.

CHOOSE an interesting object, a class pet, or an unusual plant.

LIST as many words and phrases as you can for your description, but do not name your topic. Remember to list sensory details (how things look, sound, smell, taste, feel) and to include specific, colorful nouns, verbs, and modifiers.

TRADE lists with another pair of students, and try to **FIGURE OUT** what their list describes. Then try to think of words to **ADD** to their list.

Bouncing Basketballs . . . . Descriptive Writing (5)

■ **LIST** as many words and phrases as you can to describe a room in your school (classroom, gym, cafeteria, etc.). Remember to list sensory details (how things look, sound, smell, taste, feel) and to include specific, colorful nouns, verbs, and modifiers.

Remember and Remember . . . . Narrative Writing (4)

■ **REMEMBER** a big holiday you celebrated—a day that was special and fun. **MAKE** two lists of details about the day: one list of details you would include if you were writing to a friend, and a second list of details you would include if writing to an older relative, such as a grandparent. (Some details may be on both lists, but try to think of special details that would be interesting to each reader.)

That's a different story. . . . . Narrative Writing (5)

■ Narrative writing is writing that tells a story, but different kinds of people like different kinds of stories.
THINK of two people you know who are very different, such as your little brother and your grandmother.
SEARCH your handbook for a sample story that one of them would like very much, but the other one might not like.
WRITE a paragraph telling which story you chose, who your two readers are, and why one would like it and the other might not.

Running into . . . . Writing Basic Sentences (4)

■ **WRITE** three run-on sentences about things running into each other.
Example: Dad backed our car into our doghouse the dog began barking.
EXCHANGE your run-on sentences and **CORRECT** them. If you need help, see handbook page 115.

And so on, and so on . . . Writing Basic Sentences (5)

■ **FIND** a very short news article (two or three paragraphs) in a newspaper.
COPY the article onto a sheet of paper, leaving out all the end
punctuation and initial capital letters. Add the word "and" in each
place where a sentence ended. In other words, make the article into
one long, rambling sentence.
Now **TRADE** papers with a classmate who has done the same thing.
CORRECT each other's rambling sentences. If you need help, see
handbook page 115.
Finally, **COMPARE** your corrected sentences with the original article.
Your sentences don't have to match the article exactly, as long as they
are correct and the meaning is clear.

Combo Challenge . . . . Combining Sentences (4)

■ **WRITE** three short sentences about the illustration on handbook page 118.
CHALLENGE a partner to combine your sentences, using any of the
techniques on pages 119-121 to make one smoother, detailed sentence.

Make it flow, bro. . . . . Combining Sentences (5)

■ **WRITE** at least five short, choppy sentences about one of your favorite
stories. **TRADE** papers with a partner.
USE the techniques on handbook pages 119-121 to combine some of each
other's sentences.

You've got to please yourself. . . Writing with Style (4)

■ **READ** about developing a sense of style on handbook page 123.
EXPLAIN to a partner what this statement means: "Writing without
details is like baking cookies without flour."

Coming to Terms . . . . Writing with Style (5)

■ **HUNT** for answers on handbook pages 129-131 in your handbook to complete the following definitions.

1. Checking a final draft for errors is

_____.

2. A story from a writer's life is a

_____.

3. Words that help tie ideas together in your writing are

_____.

4. Sharing ideas in groups to collect a variety of thoughts on a subject is

_____.

The Forms of Writing

A Very Bad-Good Day .... Writing in Journals (4)

■ **THINK** about your best and worst days.
   DIVIDE a fresh page in your journal into two columns.
   LABEL one "Best Day" and the other "Worst Day." (You may want to draw a smiling face over one column and a frowning face over the other.)
   LIST details about each day in the appropriate column.
   USE this page to generate a comparison/contrast paragraph in the future.

I know just how she felt. .... Writing in Journals (5)

■ **READ** "The Alley Dog" on handbook page 244.
   WRITE a journal entry telling your response to the poem. Write about how the poem made you feel, if it reminds you of someone or something in your own life, and so on.

Who am I? .... Writing Personal Narratives (4)

■ **BEGIN** a collection box for writing topics. (You'll need a small box or container.)
   PERSONALIZE the box by decorating it. Add to its contents regularly—movie-ticket stubs, letters or cards from relatives, photographs, found items, anything that represents you and your life.
   KEEP your collection growing and use it as a treasure chest of writing ideas.

Listen, my friend. .... Writing Personal Narratives (5)

■ **THINK** of an important event in your life.
   SHARE the story of this event in a letter to your best friend. Use the handbook chapters on "Writing Personal Narratives" and "Friendly Notes and Letters" to help you as you write.
   GIVE your story a catchy title. Here are some ideas:

   I Saved the Day   Grandpa's Fishy Fish Story

   Four Aunts in One Kitchen   My Sister's Crazy Plan

Dear Occupant,........... Friendly Notes and Letters (4)

■ Have you ever received mail addressed just to you? Have you sent letters to friends or family members recently?
    LIST the people you have written to or would like to write to. Keep it general (friend, cousin, grandparent, aunt, and so on).
    MAKE a list of all the reasons to write to them.
    Then **TURN** to handbook page 144. Did you list any of the reasons you find there?

E-xciting .... Friendly Notes and Letters (5)

■ It's fun to send and receive electronic mail!
    THINK of someone you would like to send an e-mail message to.
    REVIEW handbook pages 146-147 and write your message.
    SEND it electronically if possible, or by snail mail if necessary.

What's so special?............... Biographical Writing (4)

■ **THINK** of someone you know who is special and interesting.
    WRITE DOWN the person's name and three things you would include in a biographical sketch about the person.

In the Spotlight .... Biographical Writing (5)

■ **THINK** of a person in history who would make a good subject for a biographical sketch.
    WRITE a short paragraph telling two things that make this person special, and two things that you would like to know about the person.

For the Record............. Writing Newspaper Stories (4)

■ Using the tips on handbook page 159 for interviewing, **PREPARE** a list of questions to ask someone that you find interesting.
    If possible, **INTERVIEW** that person and **PUBLISH** your interview (with permission) in the school paper or newsletter.

Big News .... Writing Newspaper Stories (5)

■ **REVIEW** the three types of newspaper stories on handbook page 157.
THINK about things that have happened in your school and city recently.
WRITE down a real event for each type of newspaper story: a news story, a feature story, and a letter to the editor. **WRITE** a headline for each story.

A stitch in time . . . . Writing Book Reviews (4)

■ **RECALL** a favorite folktale or fable.
WRITE answers to the following questions:
1. What do you think the author wants you to learn from the story?
2. What happens in the story that leads you to believe this is the author's message?
SHARE your review of the story with your classmates.

In a Nutshell .... Writing Book Reviews (5)

■ **READ** the sample book review on handbook page 167.
WRITE a "mini-review" of the last book or story you read.
WRITE one sentence that answers each of these questions: What is the story about? What do I like about this story? What is the story's theme or message?

Quadrilateral .... How-To Writing (4)

■ **DRAW** a picture of a simple shape. On a separate piece of paper, **WRITE** an explanation of how to draw the shape, without naming it.
EXCHANGE papers with a partner. (Keep the drawing hidden from view until after your partner has tried to draw the shape.) If your explanation is clear, your drawings will be similar.

That's disgusting! .... How-To Writing (5)

■ **WRITE** a paragraph explaining how to make something or do something that sounds "yucky" but is actually fun, delicious, or both.
USE "Eating Dirt" on handbook page 172 as a model.

"For Matt" . . . . Business Writing (4)

- ■ **WRITE** a short business letter to a local community official asking for information about an upcoming event, a building project, or something else related to business in your area or city.
    USE your own paper or write your letter on a computer. Follow the format on handbook page 179.

Don't forget. . . . . Business Writing (5)

- ■ Do you know someone who is always forgetting something? Does your mom forget where she put her keys? Does your friend forget to return things he borrows?
    WRITE a memo to remind someone about something. (If there's something you often forget, write a memo to yourself.)
    FOLLOW the format on handbook page 183.

In summary . . . . Writing a Summary (4-5)

- ■ **SELECT** a short article from a newspaper or magazine. **MASK** its title. Then **EXCHANGE** articles with a partner. **READ** the "Big Squeeze" on handbook page 185 to help you decide on the main idea.
    WRITE your own title for the article and compare it to the actual one. Did you find the main idea?

Recess rocks! . . . . Writing Observation Reports (4)

- ■ **TAKE** your notebook with you when you go outside for recess.
    RECORD the sights, sounds, smells, and physical sensations you notice for 10 minutes.
    WRITE a short report that includes the sensory data you collected.
    READ your recess report to your class.

Sharpened Senses . . . . . Writing Observation Reports (5)

- ■ Can you write an observation report with your eyes closed? Sure you can! **FIND** a place with lots of activity.
    SIT DOWN, CLOSE YOUR EYES, and **TAKE NOTES** (it's okay if they're scribbly; write big) about everything you hear, smell, touch, feel, and taste. Use your notes to **WRITE** an observation report.

Nitty "Griddy" . . . . Writing a Classroom Report (4)

■ **GET STARTED** on writing a report.
MAKE a gathering grid for any topic you find interesting. (Use the sample grid on handbook page 195.)
INCLUDE questions that you would like answered.
KEEP the grid handy and **FILL** it in as you learn more about your topic.

Going Batty . . . . Writing a Classroom Report (5)

■ **MAKE** a cluster like the one on handbook page 193. In the center circle, write the topic "bats."
COMPLETE the cluster by writing some interesting questions about bats. Finally, **CHOOSE** one question you would most like to answer in a report, and **PUT** a star next to it. Keep your cluster; you might use it someday!

Shooting Star . . . . Writing Fantasies (4)

■ Using your favorite colored pencil or pen, **WRITE** your favorite wish in the middle of a blank sheet of paper. Then **SURROUND** the wish with ideas about everything that would happen if the wish came true.
USE your cluster to write a fantasy based on your wish.

Just pretend. . . . . Writing Fantasies (5)

■ Characters in fantasies often are true to life in most ways, but have one special ability—something real people or animals can't do.
CREATE a main character for a fantasy story.
LIST at least 10 things about the character (for example, name, age, appearance) and **INCLUDE** one special ability that marks the character as a fantasy character.

He lassoed Texas! . . . . Writing Tall Tales (4)

■ **SEARCH** your favorite tall tale for sentences that exaggerate. (See "A Tall Cast of Characters" on handbook page 218 for a list of the kinds of sentences to search for.)
SHARE the sentences in class.
DISCUSS why they are good examples of exaggeration.

You're incredible! . . . . Writing Tall Tales (5)

■ **IMAGINE** that you are the main character in a tall tale. **THINK** of something special you have done. Then **EXAGGERATE** it so that it becomes the main event in a tall tale.

> **WRITE** a sentence or two telling the main idea of your tall tale. Here's an example: "My little sister is always getting lost. Last week I rode my bike all the way to South America looking for her, and I finally found her in Peru."

Deposit another quarter. . . . . Writing Realistic Stories (4)

■ Work with a partner to **CREATE** an imaginary phone conversation between two of your favorite cartoon characters.

> **MAKE** this conversation sound as realistic as possible.
> **PERFORM** it for your classmates.

Get real. . . . . Writing Realistic Stories (5)

■ **CREATE** the setting for a realistic story. Set your story in a place you know well, such as your home, neighborhood, or school.

> **WRITE** a paragraph describing the setting.
> **INCLUDE** details about interesting sights, sounds, smells, and feelings.

Westward Ho! . . . . Writing Stories from History (4)

■ **PRETEND** that you are a pioneer packing for a trek on the Oregon Trail. (See handbook page 228.)

> **MAKE** a list of all the things you would take along to help you survive. Then **CROSS OUT** any item on your list that would not have been available in the 1830's. What do you have left?

Way-Back Machine . . . . . . Writing Stories from History (5)

■ **SKIM** your history book (and your own knowledge of history) to find ideas for stories from history.

> **WRITE** down one person, one event, one time period, and one place that would make a good starting point for a story. For each idea, **WRITE** a sentence telling why it would be a good story subject.

"Exit, stage right!" . . . . Writing Plays (4)

■ **BECOME** a playwright! All you need to get started is at least two characters, a problem, and a place (a setting) for the action.
　　USE the collection sheet on handbook page 234 to help you get started.
　　SAVE your ideas in your writing folder for future development.

"The raccoon did it!" . . . . Writing Plays (5)

■ **TRY** your hand at playwriting.
　　READ acts 1 and 2 of the play on handbook pages 233 and 237.
　　Then **WRITE** the final act. How does it all turn out? Will Dad discover his broken fishing rod and blame someone who's innocent? You decide!

Color me glad. . . . . Writing Poems (4)

■ **READ** "Purple Poems" on handbook page 241.
　　WRITE a color poem of your own.

Prose into Poetry . . . . Writing Poems (5)

■ **TAKE** something you have written—a descriptive paragraph or a story, for example—and **TURN** it into a poem. **USE** some of the devices explained in "The Sounds of Poetry." (**SEE** handbook page 245.) The samples on pages 242-244 show you how it's done.

Why is a ___ like a ___ ? . . . . Writing Riddles (4-5)

■ **LOOK** at the "Crack Up" riddles on handbook page 251. They use words that sound alike, and are sometimes even spelled alike, but have different meanings.
　　EXPLAIN the meaning of each word in the pairs below.
　　USE a dictionary to help you. (Answers will vary.)

1. star/star	**3.** knight/night	**5.** brush/brush
2. pain/pane	**4.** aisle/isle	**6.** beau/bow

Challenge: **WRITE** a riddle using one or more of the word pairs above.

The Tools of Learning

Bookworm . . . . Using the Library (4)

- **DRAW** a simple map of your library.
  INCLUDE these items: the spot where you can usually find the librarian, card catalog (or computer-catalog terminals), checkout desk, novels, biographies, nonfiction books, reference books, magazines, and new books.
  SHOW your work to your teacher and librarian.

Snooping Around . . . . Using the Library (5)

- **VISIT** the reference section of your school library. Browse the shelves to **FIND** three books that you have not used before that could help you with your assignments. **WRITE** down the title of each book and a sentence telling how it can help you. **KEEP** this information to refer to the next time you have a research assignment.

Logging On . . . . Using the Internet (4-5)

- **VISIT** the Write Source Web site.
  FIND the address in the handbook chapter "Using the Internet."
  Then **GO** to two research links that sound interesting. **WRITE** down the addresses of the links and a short description of what you find there. **KEEP** this information to refer to the next time you have a research assignment.

Feelings . . . . Using Reading Strategies (4)

- **ANSWER** these questions in your reading journal for the last book you read on your own: What were your feelings after reading the opening chapter(s) of this book? After reading half of the book? After finishing the book?
  KEEP these "before, during, and after" questions handy while reading your next book. You may want to share your responses with a reading partner or group.

KWL . . . . Using Reading Strategies (5)

■ **REVIEW** handbook page 273 for an explanation and example of KWL (Know, Want, Learn).

Then **GRAB** any textbook you have and **TURN** to a chapter you haven't read yet.

USE the strategy to read the chapter you turned to.

A picture is worth . . . . Reading Graphics (4)

■ **INVENT** new symbols for the top three signs on handbook page 281.

USE your imagination!

TRY OUT your new symbols on several friends. Did they understand your messages?

Everybody line up. . . . . Reading Graphics (5)

■ **REVIEW** the line diagram on handbook page 282.

Then **MAKE** a line diagram showing a different group of animals, such as warm-blooded animals, rain-forest animals, or Arctic animals.

USE your science book or a reference book if you need help.

They're related. . . . . Building Vocabulary Skills (4)

■ **SUBSTITUTE** better words for the "lazy" words that are underlined in each sentence below. (Check out "Use a Thesaurus" on handbook page 292 for information about finding the right word.)

1. The old car's old tires needed repair.
2. A bicyclist goes by, and a squirrel runs across the road.
3. Elsie walks to the big grocery store.

Now **WRITE** sentences with "lazy" words of your own and **ASK** a partner to revise them.

A What-ologist? . . . . Building Vocabulary Skills (5)

■ Each of the following words is built from roots found in your handbook's list of word roots, beginning on page 298.

LIST the words below on a sheet of paper, **FIND** the roots in the handbook list, and **WRITE** down what you think each "ologist" does. **USE** a dictionary to check and correct your work.

audiologist	pathologist	toxicologist
dermatologist	psychologist	zoologist

"BRrrr" in FeBRuary . . . . Becoming a Better Speller (4-5)

■ **INVENT** sayings to help you and your classmates remember how to spell the months of the year or another list of tricky spelling words.

MAKE UP sayings for four or five of the months you find the hardest to spell. (See the strategies on handbook page 307 for help.)

POST the most helpful sayings near the calendar in your classroom.
Example: JanuAry has cold Air!

Bravo! . . . . Giving Speeches (4-5)

■ **CHOOSE** a favorite experience or event that you can tell about in 2 to 3 minutes.

WRITE down each thing that happened during this experience on separate note cards.

PUT the cards in order and **MEMORIZE** them all.

PRACTICE telling about your experience until you don't need the cards anymore.

Then **TELL** the story to your group or class.

Mime Time . . . . Performing Poems (4)

■ **FIND** a short poem that "shows" a lot of action.

ASK a partner to read the poem while you **PANTOMIME** the action lines.

PRACTICE the poem until your timing is perfect and then **PERFORM** it for an audience.

Flamingo Flamenco .... Performing Poems (5)

■ **SCORE** the poem "Flamingo of Spring" on handbook page 318 as if you were going to perform it with a partner. **FOLLOW** the format on page 321.

5 W's and H .... Improving Viewing Skills (4)

■ **CHOOSE** a television news program and **WATCH** at least one complete story. While watching, **TAKE** a few notes on the story, using the 5 W's and H on handbook page 325.
REPORT the story to your class. (You and your classmates could plan a regular "news hour" of your own.)

Be aware. .... Improving Viewing Skills (5)

■ **WRITE** a paragraph analyzing a TV commercial. Tell what the product is, the selling method used in the commercial, and what viewers should "be aware" of. (**SEE** handbook page 328.)

Telephone .... Improving Listening Skills (4)

■ **PLAY** the game "telephone" with your group or class.
BEGIN by giving the directions for getting from your bedroom to the refrigerator, or any other object in your house.
WHISPER them to the next person "on the line." The last person in the game should repeat your directions aloud. Are they accurate? If not, review "Becoming a Good Listener" on handbook page 331, and **TRY** again.

It's a dirty job. .... Improving Listening Skills (5)

■ **DO** this minilesson with a partner. **REVIEW** the listening tips on handbook page 331. **PRACTICE** using them while your partner reads "Eating Dirt" (page 172) aloud. Then **TRY** to tell your partner all the steps in making "dirt."
If your partner wants to practice listening, **READ** one of the samples on pages 174-175.

Getting It Together . . . . Using Graphic Organizers (4)

■ **USE** the "5 W's Organizer" on handbook page 334 to organize information about a class party or school event you'd like to have.
Then **WRITE** a sample invitation.

Back to Camp . . . . Using Graphic Organizers (5)

■ **READ** "Camp Knollwood" on handbook page 104.
USE two different graphic organizers (**SEE** pages 334-335) to take notes on the sample.
NOTICE how your two sets of notes are different, and how they are the same.

First-Letter Fun . . . . Thinking and Writing (4)

■ **CREATE** a memory device, using the first letter of each of the six important types of thinking on handbook page 345.
Examples: Randy Utters "Ahem!" Anytime Squeak Escapes.
AS "U" ARE

Now **WRITE** your own silly sentence or other memory device to help you remember the categories.

Just the Facts, Ma'am . . . . Thinking and Writing (5)

■ **LIST** the things you know about a favorite wild animal.
Then **LOOK UP** your topic in several reference books.
PLACE a check mark in front of the factual statements in your list.
USE these facts to write a paragraph about your topic. See "Tips for Understanding" on handbook page 340 to help you organize your paragraph.

Working It Out . . . . Thinking Clearly (4-5)

■ **THINK** about a big problem you need to solve or have recently solved.
CONSIDER the guidelines on handbook page 351 and answer the questions in your journal.
SAVE the page for a handy reference whenever you face a new problem.

"I never knew that." .... Writing as a Learning Tool (4)

■ **READ** "Help Save Our Manatees" on handbook page 98.
WRITE a learning-log entry that tells your thoughts and feelings about the essay.

Get the picture. .... Writing as a Learning Tool (5)

■ **THINK** about a story that you know well and like a lot.
DRAW a picture of something from the story that you remember very well, such as the setting, a character, or an event.

Goal to Go .... Completing Assignments (4)

■ **IDENTIFY** three goals you would like to reach by the end of this school year.
In your journal, **WRITE** each goal on a separate page. As you work toward your goals, **RECORD** the steps you take to accomplish them.
GIVE yourself a reward when you reach a goal, and **TELL** at least one other person about it.

Sticking to a Schedule .... Completing Assignments (5)

■ **USE** handbook page 358 to make a weekly planner for yourself, or use a printed form.
CHALLENGE yourself to stick with it.
At the end of the week, **EVALUATE** your planner. Did it help you get assignments in on time? Why or why not?

Goin' West .... Working in Groups (4)

■ **FORM** a small group (three to five students) and **PRETEND** that you are part of a wagon train heading to California in 1848. Winter has come early, and your group must decide whether to stop where you are, or keep moving. (You may add any details you want to make this scenario more "real." Perhaps the food supply is running low, or one of the horses is limping.)
REACH a consensus on what to do, using the guidelines on handbook page 364 to help form a plan.

Story Ideas . . . . Working in Groups (5)

■ **THINK** about the last story you read, or **READ** one in the "Story and Playwriting" section of your handbook.

    USE the questions on page 365 to help you **LIST** ideas to share in a group discussion of the story. (You don't need to answer all the questions; pick four or five.)

    If possible, **SHARE** your ideas in a small-group discussion of the story.

Did you say "test"? . . . . Taking Tests (4)

■ After reading "Responding to Writing Prompts" on handbook page 368, **WRITE** an essay-test question and its answer for a science topic that you are studying now.

    SHARE it with your study group or class.

Key Questions . . . . Taking Tests (5)

■ **REVIEW** the key words on handbook page 368.

    WRITE a sample prompt (essay-test question) for each key word. For ideas, **THINK** about topics you are studying.

Learning As I Go . . . . Taking Good Notes (4)

■ **KEEP** a "learning log" for a week. (You may use several pages of your journal or notebook.)

    Using handbook page 375, **TAKE** notes in each of your classes. What did you do? What did you learn? What ideas do you have for doing tomorrow's assignments?

    At the end of the week, **EVALUATE** your notes' usefulness. How did they help you learn?

Notes on Notes . . . . Taking Good Notes (5)

■ **DO** this minilesson with a partner.

    BRAINSTORM and **LIST** situations in which good note-taking skills would be a big help.

    THINK about things that come up in and out of school, and also about things that will come up in the future.

Proofreader's Guide

Short Change .... Period (4)

■ **LIST** three different ways periods are used in the following sentences, besides at the end of each. Then **CHECK** handbook page 377 to see how you did.
1. I might as well change my name to I. M. Short.
2. I only have $4.93, and I owe my neighbor $5.75.
3. When I tell her my problem, Ms. Jackson will not be happy.

So Much to Do .... Period (5)

■ **STUDY** handbook page 377. Then **CLOSE** your book. **LIST** the five ways in which periods are used, and **GIVE** an example of each.

Commas by Committee .... Comma (4)

■ **FORM** a group of five or six students. Working together, **SEARCH** your handbook to **FIND** examples of all the ways to use a comma. (**SEE** pages 379-381.) Divide up the work by having each group member find examples of two or three different ways to use commas.

  COPY each example sentence and the page number where you found it.

  LABEL each example to tell how commas are used. Group members who finish quickly can help those who are still searching. Finally, **GLUE** all your examples onto poster board to make a comma collage.

The Story on Commas .... Comma (5)

■ **WRITE** a story about an imaginary garage sale.

  TELL about where it was held, who came, what was sold, and so on. Make your story true to life or a fantasy. (What if animals had a garage sale?)

  USE commas in as many different ways as you can. (**SEE** pages 379-381.)

Connect those clauses. . . . . Semicolon (4)

■ **REWRITE** the two example sentences next to "Between Two Independent Clauses" on handbook page 380.
USE a semicolon instead of a comma and conjunction to connect the clauses.
Then **WRITE** one more sentence using a semicolon correctly.

Lessons Learned . . . . Semicolon (5)

■ **TURN** to the sample narrative paragraph on handbook page 79.
REWRITE three sentences from the paragraph, each time using a semicolon to replace a comma and a coordinating conjunction.

It's about time. . . . . Colon (4)

■ **READ** about colons on handbook page 382.
Then **WRITE** three sentences that are all about times in your life (mealtimes, schooltimes, bedtimes, etc.).
USE colons correctly.

Stories, Poems, Pictures, ... Colon (5)

■ **WRITE** four sentences that list things that can be found in your handbook.
USE a colon correctly in each sentence.
Example: "Writing Poems" has samples of many kinds of poetry: free verse, haiku, ballads, limericks, and more.

Charlie's Horse . . . . Apostrophe (4)

■ **LIST** the names of four people you know and three groups (family, Girl Scouts, baseball team, etc.) you are part of. Next to each name, **WRITE** its possessive form.
(*Hint:* You'll need seven apostrophes. **SEE** handbook page 385 for details!)

Keep it short. . . . . Apostrophe (5)

- **DO** this minilesson with a partner. **STUDY** the contractions at the bottom of handbook page 384.
  Then have your partner **READ** several contractions aloud while you **WRITE** them down.
  CHECK and **CORRECT** your work; then **TRADE** roles: You read the words for your partner.

Questions . . . . . . Quotation Marks and Question Marks (4)

- **WRITE** three questions. Each question should **INCLUDE** the title of an article, an essay, a book chapter, a short story, a song, or a poem.
  Make sure to **USE** quotation marks and question marks correctly. (**SEE** handbook pages 386-387.)

"Lunch?" . . . . Quotation Marks and Question Marks (5)

- **WRITE** a short dialogue between two people who are making lunch.
  USE quotation marks and question marks correctly.

Give me an example. Capitalization (4)

- Handbook pages 389-392 present the rules for capitalization.
  WRITE one example of a word or phrase that is capitalized according to each rule. Do not write a word that is shown in your handbook.
  WORK on this with a partner if your teacher permits.

To Cap or Not to Cap . . . . Capitalization (5)

- The following words are sometimes capitalized. It depends on how the word is used in the sentence. (**SEE** handbook pages 389-392.)
  WRITE two sentences using each word: one sentence in which the word is capitalized, and one in which it is not. (Do not use the words as first words in your sentences!)

  president   mother   earth   north   white house   war

Numbers by the Rules . . . . Numbers (4)

■ **DO** this minilesson with a partner.
READ about numbers on handbook page 393.
Then **READ** page 444. Each time you come to a number, **FIGURE OUT** why it is written as it is (as a numeral or in words).

Billions and Billions of Stars . . . . Numbers (5)

■ **READ** about numbers on handbook page 393. Then **READ** page 444.
WRITE five more sentences about the solar system.
USE information from the table on page 445 or from your science book.
Make sure you **USE** numbers correctly.

Puppies on the Loose . . . . Plurals (4)

■ **IMAGINE** that your dog has six puppies. One day, while you're at school, the puppies romp through the house, destroying everything in sight.
WRITE a story about the puppies' day, using the plural forms of as many of the following words as you can. (**SEE** handbook pages 394-395.)

shoe	dish	sofa
box	paw	pillow
candy	loaf	nose

One Elf or Two? . . . . Plurals (5)

■ **READ** about plurals of nouns ending in *f* or *fe*. (**SEE** handbook page 394.)
WRITE the plurals of the following words; then **USE** a dictionary to **CHECK** and **CORRECT** your work.

| belief | half | life | self | wife |
| elf | hoof | roof | wharf | |

Taking Shortcuts . . . . Abbreviations (4)

■ **MATCH** each of the following abbreviations to the word or phrase it represents. **SEE** handbook pages 396 and 397 for help.

_____	1. Mr.	a.	et cetera (and so forth)
_____	2. Mrs.	b.	as soon as possible
_____	3. Ms.	c.	kilogram
_____	4. etc.	d.	post meridiem (after noon)
_____	5. a.m.	e.	combination of Miss and Mistress
_____	6. p.m.	f.	Mistress
_____	7. ASAP	g.	ante meridiem (before noon)
_____	8. kg	h.	Mister

Don't MTB; it's PN. . . . . Abbreviations (5)

■ Think of at least five phrases that you use all the time—"no way," "pizza night," "home before dark," "miss the bus," etc.
    TURN all your phrases into initialisms. (**CHECK** handbook page 396.)
    Examples: "miss the bus" becomes MTB; "pizza night" becomes PN.
    Now **WRITE** a paragraph using all your initialisms.
    TRADE paragraphs with a partner and **FIGURE OUT** each other's
        initialisms.

"C" Snakes . . . . Checking Your Spelling (4)

■ Certain words have letters that are pronounced like other letters. "Certain" is one of those words. The "c" makes the sound of "s." It sounds like the word should be spelled "sertain."
    On your own paper, **LIST** at least 10 other words from handbook pages
        398-401 in which a "c" makes the "s" sound.
    COMPARE papers with a classmate.

Short, but Not Simple .... Checking Your Spelling (5)

■ Short words are not always easy to spell. There may be a silent letter, or a sound that could be spelled several different ways.

LOOK for 10 three- or four-letter words in the list of commonly misspelled words on handbook pages 398-401.

CHOOSE ones that cause you trouble, and write them down. **THINK** about why each one might be easy to misspell.

WRITE a brief paragraph that uses as many of these short words as possible. **UNDERLINE** each short word that you used from your list.

ASK a partner to read your paragraph and check the spellings of your underlined words, using the list of commonly misspelled words.

On the Board .... Using the Right Word (4)

■ **FILL IN** the blanks below with either "a" or "an," whichever is correct. **CHECK** handbook page 402 for help.

1. Our classroom has _____ bulletin board.

2. Once _____ month, we put new pictures on the board.

3. We have posters of _____ eagle, _____ owl, and _____ parrot in the room.

4. Paula has _____ idea for next month's board.

5. She wants to put up _____ picture of _____ astronaut.

Who's on first?............Using the Right Word (5)

■ **FILL IN** the blanks below with either "whose" or "who's," whichever is correct. **CHECK** handbook page 411 for help.

1. _____ book is this?

2. It belongs to Jordan, _____ in my math class.

3. _____ going to the recycling center?

4. _____ turn is it to go?

5. This is Sanjeev, _____ family is from India.

6. Is he the one _____ new here?

7. _____ science class are you in?

8. My teacher is Ms. Chang, _____ from China.

On the Table..............Parts of a Sentence (4-5)

■ **REVIEW** "Parts of a Sentence—Subject, Predicate, Modifier" on handbook pages 412-413.
On a sheet of paper, **MAKE** a table with columns labeled "Subjects," "Predicates," and "Modifiers."
TURN to "Help Save Our Manatees" on page 98. **COMPLETE** your table by **WRITING** in some simple subjects, simple predicates, and modifiers from the essay. (**LIST** at least five of each.)

Free Samples...............Clauses and Phrases (4)

■ **REVIEW** "Clauses" and "Phrases" on handbook page 414.
WRITE one more example of each kind of clause and phrase discussed.

Explain this...............Clauses and Phrases (5)

■ **REVIEW** "Clauses" and "Phrases" on handbook page 414.
CLOSE your book. **WRITE** a sentence telling what a clause is; then **WRITE** an example. Do the same for a phrase.
USE your handbook to **CHECK** and **CORRECT** your work.

Whoa, Nelly . . . . Types of Sentences (4-5)

■ **OPEN** your handbook to "Saddle Up!" on page 317.
   COPY one example of each type of sentence:
   • simple sentence with simple subject and simple predicate;
   • simple sentence with simple subject and compound predicate;
   • compound sentence; and
   • complex sentence.
   (**SEE** handbook page 415.) Make sure to **LABEL** your sentences.

What kind is that? . . . . Kinds of Sentences (4-5)

■ **LOOK** at the cover of your handbook.
   WRITE a dialogue that the students in the illustration might be having.
   INCLUDE at least one sentence of each kind listed on page 416.

Who does what? . . . . Subject-Verb Agreement (4)

■ **REVIEW** subject-verb agreement on handbook page 116. On your own paper,
   COMPLETE each sentence below by adding a subject that agrees with the
   verb. **LABEL** each subject singular or plural.

   1. _____ laughs a lot.   **3.** _____ tell funny jokes.

   2. _____ write good stories.   **4.** _____ sings in a choir.

Don't be disagreeable. . . . . . . Subject-Verb Agreement (5)

■ On your own paper, **COMPLETE** the following sentences using present tense
   verbs. (**SEE** handbook page 427.) Make sure each verb agrees with its
   subject. (**SEE** page 116.)
   1. LaTonya or her brothers . . .   **3.** Our neighbor and his sons . . .
   2. The mice or the hamster . . .   **4.** The players and the coach . . .

Dr. Jeff: Dentist, Man, Runner . . . . Nouns (4)

■ **LIST** five people you know. Their names are *proper nouns*. Next to each
   name, **LIST** some *common nouns* that also "name" that person.

What am I? . . . . Nouns (5)

■ **COMPOSE** "What Am I?" riddles about two or three objects in your classroom. *Example:* I have a mouth and silver teeth that fall out everywhere. What am I? (Answer: stapler)
  SHARE your riddles with a classmate and listen to his or hers.
  LIST all the riddle answers on your own paper. **SEE** handbook page 418 for an explanation of abstract and concrete nouns. **LABEL** each noun "abstract" or "concrete." What have you discovered?

They agree! . . . . Pronouns (4)

■ **STUDY** "Agreement of Pronouns" on handbook page 421. Notice that the word "antecedent" refers to the noun that the pronoun replaces. Antecedent means "comes before." A pronoun must always have a noun that comes before it.
  SPEND several minutes writing a list of interesting nouns.
  SELECT your favorite noun from the list. Then **WRITE** a sentence using that noun and a pronoun that refers back to it.
  GET TOGETHER with two or three other students and **SHARE** sentences.
  DECIDE whether the pronoun in each sentence agrees with the noun it replaces.

Points of View . . . . Pronouns (5)

■ **STUDY** "Person of Pronouns" on handbook page 422. Then, on page 103, read the sample paragraph "Someone Who Cares."
  Working with a partner, have one person **READ** the selection, changing all the first-person references to second-person pronouns. (Make the changes as you read out loud, quietly.) Then have the other person **READ** the same selection, changing all the first-person references to third-person pronouns.
  DISCUSS how changing the point of view affects the story.

Chunky and Chewy . . . . Verbs (4)

■ **WRITE** a paragraph about your favorite food. **USE** *looks, smells, tastes,* and *feels* as linking verbs. (**SEE** handbook page 426.)

Name Dropper .... Verbs (5)

- **REVIEW** the list of irregular verbs on handbook page 429.
  FIND an irregular verb that begins with the first letter in your first or last name (or use the name of a friend or family member).
  WRITE three crazy sentences by completing the sentence starters below, using the correct form of your verb.

  1. Yesterday, I _____ .

  2. I have _____ .

  3. I will _____ .

The Monday Morning Talent Show ...... Adjectives (4)

- **REVIEW** adjectives on handbook page 430.
  TURN to "Talent Show and Tell" on page 99. From the essay, **LIST** 10 adjectives and the nouns they modify.

It's most irregular. .... Adjectives (5)

- **CHOOSE** three of the irregular adjectives listed at the top of handbook page 431. For each adjective, **WRITE** one sentence that uses all three forms: positive, comparative, and superlative. **MAKE** your sentences about things that are irregular, unusual, or strange.

Brush teeth briefly. .... Adverbs (4)

- **THINK** of four different things you do every day.
  WRITE a sentence about each one.
  In each sentence, **USE** an adverb to tell when, where, how, or how often you do the thing. (**SEE** handbook page 432.)

Right Time, Right Place .... Adverbs (5)

- **IMAGINE** that you are the sports reporter for your school newspaper.
  WRITE a short article about a game of your choice—football, baseball, or any other sport. **USE** at least one of each type of adverb shown on handbook page 432.

Whoosh! Woof! Boing! ....Interjections (4-5)

■ **LIST** as many interjections as you can that imitate sounds made by people, animals, or things. (**SEE** handbook page 433.)
Then **USE** each interjection in a sentence.

Find Festus! ....Prepositions (4)

■ **READ** about prepositions and prepositional phrases on handbook page 434. Then **TURN** to page 139 and **READ** "The Great Gerbil Escape."
FIND the prepositional phrases in the first four paragraphs of this story. **WRITE** them on your own paper. The first one has been done for you.
Paragraph 1: of gerbils, from our bathtub

Over the river and . . . .Prepositions (5)

■ **WRITE** five sentences about chasing a runaway pet.
USE at least one prepositional phrase in every sentence. (**SEE** handbook page 434.)

They stick together. ....Conjunctions (4-5)

■ Six pairs of correlative conjunctions are listed on handbook page 435.
CHOOSE four pairs. **WRITE** one sentence for each pair.

Student Almanac

Hand Signals .... Using Language (4)

◼ **LOOK** at the sign language chart on handbook page 440. In order to use this sign language well, you have to learn and practice it. Then you can only "talk" to someone who has also learned it.

> As a class, **THINK** of as many hand signals as you can that everybody already knows, such as the one for "stop." If you play (or watch) sports, **SHOW** the hand signals used in the games.

Finally, **CHOOSE** a password and have everybody in the class **LEARN** to sign it in the sign language shown in your handbook.

Updated English .... Using Language (5)

◼ **DO** this minilesson in a small group or with your whole class.

> **READ** handbook page 437.
> **ADD** a paragraph to the end of the essay telling how English has changed in recent times. Where have some of the new words come from? First **BRAINSTORM** and **LIST** ideas.

Then **TURN** your ideas into a paragraph.

Great Gaggles of Geese! .... Exploring Science (4)

◼ **LOOK** at the table of animal facts on handbook page 442.

> **WRITE** a short story about either farm animals or jungle animals.
> **CHOOSE** from the animals listed in the table, and use as many of the terms and facts from the table as you can.

In Orbit . . . . Exploring Science (5)

■ **LOOK** at "Our Solar System" on handbook page 444 and the chart on page 445.

> **WRITE** a simple question that could be answered easily with the information in one box on the chart.
>
> **WRITE** a slightly harder question that requires comparing two or more planets.
>
> Finally, **WRITE** a question for which you must compare all the planets.
>
> **SHARE** your questions with the entire class.

Times are changing. . . . . Improving Math Skills (4)

■ Jon bought a notebook for $1.89, three pencils for $.49 each, a ruler for $.97, and a ballpoint pen for $2.69. He gave the clerk $10.

> **SOLVE** this problem. How much change did he get back? (**SEE** handbook pages 452-453 for help.) Show your work.
>
> Now **WRITE** your own word problem, similar to the one above.
>
> **CHANGE** the objects and the prices. A few volunteers may put their problems on the board for discussion.

The clock strikes twelve. . . . . . Improving Math Skills (5)

■ **SOLVE** the following word problem, using the five steps explained on handbook page 452.

> A cuckoo clock has a cuckoo bird that comes out of its birdhouse and cuckoos each hour: once at one o'clock, twice at two o'clock, three times at three o'clock, and so on. How many times does the cuckoo bird cuckoo in one whole day?

Map Mysteries . . . . Using Maps (4)

■ **USE** the United States map on handbook page 461 to **SOLVE** these map mysteries:

> 1. What state touches two of the Great Lakes and the Atlantic Ocean?
> 2. What state separates the Atlantic Ocean from the Gulf of Mexico?
> 3. What state is bordered by only one other state?
> 4. What states are bordered by the Mississippi River? (It begins in Minnesota and flows into the Gulf of Mexico.)

Where in the World?...................Using Maps (5)

- **FIND** each country below on the list that begins on handbook page 469.
    WRITE down the country's latitude and longitude. **USE** them to **FIND** the
    country on the world map on page 459.
    Finally, **WRITE** a sentence describing where in the world each country is.

    Cuba   Indonesia   Peru   Saudi Arabia   Vietnam

Know your rights....................Making History (4)

- **READ** handbook page 474, "The Bill of Rights."
    CHOOSE one of the amendments that you think is very important, and
    WRITE a paragraph stating why you feel this is an important right for
    people to have.
    For help writing your paragraph, read handbook page 81. It explains
    persuasive paragraphs.

Long, Long Ago ....Making History (5)

- **OPEN** your handbook to pages 478-483. Working in small groups,
    CHOOSE one of the following centuries:
        1500's   1600's   1700's   1800's
    DISCUSS how one event from the century you chose has affected (and
    may still be affecting) people's lives.
    SHARE what you discover with the entire class. You could make your
    presentation in the form of a song, poem, newscast, story, skit, and
    so on.

Minilesson Answer Key

Process of Writing

Coming to Terms (page 234)

1. proofreading
2. personal narrative
3. transitions
4. brainstorming

Forms of Writing

Why is a ___ like a ___? (page 241)

(Answers may vary.)

1. a celestial body/a talented performer
2. suffering/a sheet of glass
3. a medieval soldier/
   the time from sunset to sunrise
4. passage separating sections of
   seats/island
5. scrub vegetation (bushes)/to apply
   a brush to
6. boyfriend/a knot formed of loops

Tools of Learning

A What-ologist? (page 244)

audiologist: studies hearing
dermatologist: studies skin
pathologist: studies disease
psychologist: studies the mind
toxicologist: studies poisons
zoologist: studies animal life

Proofreader's Guide

Short Change (page 249)

1. after an initial
2. as a decimal
3. after abbreviations

Puppies on the Loose (page 252)

shoes, boxes, candies, dishes, paws,
loaves, sofas, pillows, noses

One Elf or Two? (page 252)

beliefs, elves, halves, hoofs or
hooves, lives, roofs, selves, wharfs,
wives

Taking Shortcuts (page 253)

1. h   2. f   3. e   4. a
5. g   6. d   7. b   8. c

On the Board (page 254)

1. a   2. a   3. an, an, a
4. an   5. a, an

Who's on first? (page 255)

1. Whose   2. who's   3. Who's
4. Whose   5. whose   6. who's
7. Whose   8. who's

Find Festus! (page 259)

Paragraph 2: in your tub
Paragraph 3: over the edge, of the tub
Paragraph 4: down the heat vent, in the
    wall, beside the vent, into the vent

Student Almanac

Times are changing. (page 261)

$$\begin{array}{r} \$.49 \\ \times\ \ 3 \\ \hline \$1.47 \end{array}$$

$$\begin{array}{r} \$\ 1.89 \\ .97 \\ 2.69 \\ +\ 1.47 \\ \hline \$\ 7.02 \end{array}$$

$$\begin{array}{r} \$10.00 \\ -\ 7.02 \\ \hline \$\ 2.98 \end{array}$$

The clock strikes twelve. (page 261)

156 times

Map Mysteries (page 261)

1. New York
2. Florida
3. Maine
4. Minnesota, Wisconsin, Iowa, Illinois, Missouri, Kentucky, Arkansas, Tennessee, Mississippi, Louisiana

Where in the World? (page 262)

Cuba: 21° N, 80° W
Indonesia: 5° S, 120° E
Peru: 10° S, 76° W
Saudi Arabia: 25° N, 45° E
Vietnam: 17° N, 106° E

(Sentences will vary.)

Index

* The start-up and enrichment activities are found after each set of chapter notes.